Reviews by Cat Ellington

Books by Cat Ellington

REVIEWS BY CAT ELLINGTON: THE COMPLETE ANTHOLOGY, VOL. 1

REVIEWS BY CAT ELLINGTON: THE COMPLETE ANTHOLOGY, VOL. 2

THE MAKING OF DUAL MANIA: FILMMAKING CHICAGO STYLE

REVIEWS BY CAT ELLINGTON – THE COMPLETE ANTHOLOGY LIMITED EDITION HOLIDAY GIFT SET (BOOKS 1 & 2)

REVIEWS BY CAT ELLINGTON: THE COMPLETE ANTHOLOGY, VOL. 3

MORE IMAGINATIVE THAN ORDINARY SPEECH: THE POETRY OF CAT ELLINGTON

REVIEWS BY CAT ELLINGTON: A TRILOGY OF UNIQUE CRITIQUES #1

MEMOIRS IN GOGYOHKA: A BOOK OF SHORT POEMS AND MEMOIRS

YOU CAN QUOTE ME ON THAT: A COLLECTION
OF QUOTES BY CAT ELLINGTON

REVIEWS BY CAT ELLINGTON: THE COMPLETE
ANTHOLOGY, VOL. 4

Reviews by Cat Ellington
The Complete Anthology, Vol. 4

Cat Ellington
With
Naras Kimono

Quill Pen Ink Publishing
THE BEAUTY OF EXPRESSION™
CHICAGO

Copyright ©2020 Cat Ellington

PAPERBACK ISBN-13: 978-1-7334421-5-2

Library of Congress Control Number: 2022362729

All rights reserved. No part of this publication may be reproduced or transmitted in any form or by any means electronic, including photocopy, recording, or any information storage and retrieval system, without permission in writing from the copyright owner.

Cover design: Hues of the Reviews
Vol. 4 Hue: Pouty Pumpkin
The Cat Ellington Literary Collection

Published by Quill Pen Ink Publishing
Chicago, Illinois, USA

Quill Pen Ink Publishing, 2020

Printed in the U.S.A.

Dedication

To Joyce Jackson—
For the good times, the laughs,
and the best R&B hits and dusties

Preface

Dearest reader,

I'm back, this time with the fourth installment in the Reviews by Cat Ellington series. Much like its predecessors, Volume 4, in Pouty Pumpkin, gets down to the nitty-gritty of some of the most notable works of fiction in recent years. And I had a ball composing each review in the wake of completing the respective novel to which it corresponds. Quite a few of those tales featured in this installment were gifted to me as complimentary copies on behalf of their publishers in exchange for my honest review, and on behalf of Quill Pen Ink Publishing, I thank them. It has been an honor to make the acquaintance of many new authors as the result of this action.

As you embark upon Book 4 in the series, dear reader, it is my greatest hope that you will enjoy the next volume of examinations from the Cat Ellington Literary Collection as much as I enjoyed writing them. And while a few of my analyses may present as rather brief due to other creative obligations I had during the time of their composition, nevertheless, I do hope that you will still find them informative and enjoyable to view. Thank you for your support of this, my latest contribution to the field of literature. I greatly appreciate all of you.

Lovingly,

Cat Ellington

Acknowledgments

As always, I honor my Lord and my God with the firstfruits of my praise: for were it not for him, none of this could or would be. Thank you, Heavenly Father. I love and commend you with my entire being.

Joe, Nathaniel, Nairobi, and Naras, I love y'all so much. Thank you for being there with and for me through it all. I'm so proud of all of you.

Freddie and Maurice, Lord knows I love you both – and so very deeply. Thank you for everything you do. I will never forget how great a blessing you two have been to my family and me. Not ever. Thank you.

Thank you to every team player at Goodreads, Amazon, BookBub, AUTHORSdb, BookLikes, Humanmade, Hometown Reads, LibraryThing, and Open Library for assisting us with the Cat Ellington bibliography. You always have my appreciation.

And thank you to all of my readers who find joy in my creative writing. My love and gratitude are beyond expression.

Introduction

We're on book four in the Reviews by Cat Ellington series already?! Wow! Oh my God! Golly gee! Or is it "Gee golly?" Oh, whatever the expression may be, we made it this far. And I'm so excited. I'm excited for the following reasons: (1) we've advanced to the next phase of literary criticism in the ongoing series, and (2) this volume features bonus material by Naras Kimono, a new young writer with whom I collaborated to highlight some of her writings from a few years back, writings that she composed when she was only eleven years old.

In addition to my examinations of works of fiction by Ashley Fontainne (*Whispered Pain*), Claire Seeber (*The Stepmother*), Carl Hiaasen (*Tourist Season*), B.A. Paris (*Behind Closed Doors*), Bianca Sloane (*Live to Tell*), and Fiona Davis (*The Address*), among many others, I have also elected to showcase some of Naras' reviews, including her critiques of *Dog Facts* by Joan Palmer and *Dachshunds* by Lynn M. Stone. I am tremendously proud of her as she has been given a similar gift to my own, which is that of writing. And I figured that adding some of her work here would be a great blessing to her; therefore, I did so. Thank you, Naras, for your assistance. I love you, baby.

My dearest readers, I do hope that you'll have fun with the fourth installment of Reviews by Cat Ellington. And thank you again for viewing.

Table of Contents

Dedication

Preface

Acknowledgments

Introduction

Chapter 1: Mind Games

Chapter 2: Mayhem

Chapter 3: Lies and Deceit

Chapter 4: Criminality

Chapter 5: Destruction

Chapter 6: Falsehoods

Bonus Material by Naras Kimono

Coming Soon: Reviews by Cat Ellington: The Complete Anthology, Vol. 5

About the Authors

Chapter 1
Mind Games

Cat Ellington's Review of Influence by Chris Parker

My rating: 4 out of 5 stars

Date read: August 2016

POWER DRAIN ON THE BRAIN.

After reading the synopsis for Chris Parker's *Influence*, my interest was immediately piqued. And after I went on to read some of the lovely 5-star reviews of which it served as the recipient, I decided to purchase the narrative, to find out for myself whether or not it truly lived up to all of the praise. Well, the storyline commenced just a bit too slowly for my taste, but I continued to follow it nonetheless. And in all due time, Parker's vision came alive, even to the point where it commanded my full attention, providing me with a sufficient enough reason to conclude it.

The con—as opposed to the pro—here is that Chris Parker felt the need to exaggerate the details of each character's life, causing his script to become somewhat of an annoyance to read. But overall, the talented author still reached his goal, and that's saying something.

A mystery thriller with a sprinkling of suspense, *Influence* is completely capable of entertaining any enthusiast of its respective subgenre. And while uninteresting at the outset, the mystery of its true nature soon makes a good enough effort to grab the reader, daring the same to guess whodunit. Also, as this effort is infused with many gruesome scenes, I would strongly recommend that those given to faintheartedness proceed with caution.

Chris Parker did his job with *Influence*. And were it not for such a sluggish start to the composition, I would have dared to render it a five-star rating.

Happy reading, all.

Cat Ellington's Review of Whispered Pain by Ashley Fontainne

My rating: 5 out of 5 stars

Date read: August 2016

MOMMY-TO-BE.

    Ashley Fontainne transports the reader to an uncharacteristically cold and snowy Little Rock, Arkansas where we make the acquaintance of our leading lady, 39-year-old Angie Benson, as she grows into the third semester of her first pregnancy. A nurse married to a successful attorney, Angie now spends her days at home on rest after a near miscarriage. And though she's been taking it easy for the most part, Angie does allow herself to do a little yoga just to keep fit in the best way she knows how. Her body is changing as is natural for any woman during pregnancy, and her mind has decided to take full advantage of the situation, tempting her to think that her adoring husband no longer finds her as sexy as he once had among other things. But Angie fights away the thoughts, telling herself that it's only the "pregnancy hormones" talking because they've nothing else better to do. And with that, she carries on. She's going to be a mom! And she's both nervous and excited, which is only natural.

Angie's wealthy parents, Dr. Jerome and Annette Langford, respectively, are just as thrilled at the little bundle growing in their eldest daughter's womb, especially Annette (still recovering from the death of Angie's younger sister, Amelia, 30 years ago) who insists on tending to Angie's every need during the latter's high-risk pregnancy. Amelia's death has changed the family, yes, but they continue to carry on, striving to maintain a strong bond despite it all.

As Angie reminisces about the old days, her thoughts are interrupted by the reality that she and Drake are fresh out of yogurt and blueberries—the only foods her finicky fetus craves—and her prenatal vitamins; therefore, they must go to the store to replenish those simple necessities. However, there is only one problem: an angry storm is expected to drop at least one foot of snow on their parts, and it's moving in fast. So if they're gonna head out for groceries and vitamins, they had better get a move on. Angie thinks to herself about her prenatal vitamins: *Didn't she just have them refilled?* Angie's mind is playing tricks on her perhaps?
Despite the unforgiving storm rolling in, Drake, nevertheless, agrees to head out to the store while Angie stays home to rest. How sweet.
The Bensons have it all: great jobs, good money, a huge and lovely home, luxury vehicles, and a brand new baby on the way. Everything is right with the world. Or is it?

THE AGENT OF CHAOS ARRIVES.

It's all smooth sailing, or should I say *skiing*, until the devil gets busy. Just as Drake is leaving the house to head to the store before the snow begins to pour down, he receives two calls from two very annoying people: his mother-in-law Annette, and Mrs. Williamson, a client in severe distress. On top of it all, Angie is suddenly awakened from her sleep by excruciating pain in her abdomen. Her water has broken prematurely, and time stands stock still in the presence of fear.

Yogurt, blueberries, and other necessities forgotten, Drake must get his laboring wife to the hospital as soon as possible as they're running out of time. And with nothing more important than their present situation to deal with, Drake helps Angie get dressed and out the door, they go – with panic in hot pursuit. And because the two humans don't know how to resist it, the spirit of panic takes the opportunity to rouse them up while they're on the treacherous roads driving by way of strife. It's the perfect setting for the agent of chaos who makes his entry here. All he has to do is tempt both people to take their eyes off the snowy road ahead of them. And when they do, he strikes, unleashing a dose of deadly venom in two particular forms: a patch of slick road and a grove of trees.

AM I DEAD OR ALIVE?

As Angie lays in her comatose state, only her thoughts can soothe her. She can hear their voices clearly but she can't respond. Her baby. *Where is her baby?* Her husband. *Where is her husband? Where is Drake?* She's cold, so cold, but alive. She can hear them, *all of them. They wanted her gone. They wanted her baby, her baby girl.* Angie remembers now. But Angie continues to play the role of a vegetable lest they destroy her. *Lest they kill her slowly ... and painfully.*

A LITTLE GOES A LONG WAY.

Co-starring in this fleeting psychological thriller brimming with deceit, murder, and a dollop of mental illness is none other than a small ensemble of gifted performers who shine and do their earthly creator proud, including:

- Dr. Jerome Langford, Angie's long-suffering father. Once a very happy man prominent in high society, Dr. Jerome Langford now stands in the dark shadows of his wife's manic depression – a condition only made worse by the death of their youngest daughter, Amelia.

- Annette Langford, Angie's adoring, though extremely troubled, mother.

- Miriam Stephens, Angie's attentive aunt, and Annette's cherished sister. Also married to a doctor—one Clifford Stephens, respectfully—Miriam is pulling teeth trying to hold the family together.

- Kevin Stephens, a successful funeral home director, son of Dr. Clifford and Miriam Stephens, and Angie's beloved and loyal cousin.

- Dr. Packard, Angie's primary doctor-on-call.

- Lita Kendrick, a caring nurse at St. Vincent's hospital, Angie's trusted colleague, and a sight for Drake Benson's sore eyes.

- Winton Brewer, an office worker at Turnage Wrecker Service, an aspiring teacher, and a godsend to Angie.

- Amy Kendrick, the love of Winton Brewer's life and Lita's younger sister

Joined by a pinch of bit players that would include Dr. William Hope, the head of Neurology at St. Vincent's hospital, this cast is sensational! And I enjoyed their performances immensely.

TALENT SO COMMENDABLE.

New to the literature of Ashley Fontainne, I must say that I am overtly amazed by the exceptional job the author has done with the riveting and remarkably deceptive thriller that is *Whispered Pain*.

Greatly blessed with both a gifted cast and razor-sharp dialogue that is stinging, frigid, and commanding of respect, the narrative is difficult to take even a 15-minute break from as it draws the reader into one helluva twisted plot exuding with insidious murder and deceptive mayhem.

Quite grand for a novella of 86 pages, *Whispered Pain* is one of the best short stories I've ever had the pleasure of reading. And it is my genuine pleasure to thank RMSW Publishing for the complimentary copy. Congratulations, Ashley! For yours is an exceptional talent.

Five just-when-you-thought-I-was-dead stars.

Cat Ellington's Review of Thaddeus Murfee (Thaddeus Murfee Legal Thrillers #0) by John Ellsworth

My rating: 5 out of 5 stars

Date read: August 2016

BIG BROTHER IS WATCHING. LITERALLY.

Brand spanking new law grad, Thaddeus Murfee, is about to be made an offer he can't refuse: a shadowy job with the U.S. Attorney's office in Washington D.C.

It all started with a visit from an agent with the FBI. The man showed up at the cheap apartment Thaddeus shared with three of his fellow law students and invited him into the hallway for a private talk. Flashing his FBI badge, the secretive agent queried as to whether the young man who stood before him was Thaddeus Murfee. And once the twenty-three-year-old law grad nervously answered that he was, the agent commenced explaining his visit. The U.S. Attorney wanted Thaddeus' résumé, could Thaddeus have it ready in an hour? Yes, Thaddeus could. Of course, the young lawyer was worried: *Was he in trouble? Had he done something wrong? Why was he being visited by the FBI?* It was only natural for Thaddeus to have such concerns, but in all actuality, he had absolutely nothing to worry about. As the agent explained to him, the agency had gotten Thaddeus's name from the Georgetown Law employment office, Thaddeus graduated third in his class, and they deemed him the perfect candidate for the job. They needed his résumé, could he have it ready in one hour? Yes, Thaddeus could. The face-to-face interview was in a week.

THE THIRST IS REAL.

Clad in a borrowed suit, Thaddeus Murfee, young lawyer extraordinaire, arrives at the Attorney General's office in Washington, D.C. for the sit-down interview with a group of political bigwigs, including Melissa McGrant, a mannish Assistant U.S. Attorney and native New Yorker, Harold Stuttermeyer, the Chief of Staff of the U.S. Attorney's office and top specialist in cyber-surveillance and wire-tapping, and Naomi Ranski, an African-American agent with the Federal Bureau of Investigations – who just so happens to also be an individual full of machismo, despite her being a woman, and a human soul seeker.

These three people *know* Thaddeus Murfee's story. He's a twenty-three-year-old prime for the job at hand: a kid from a broken home, no family, destitute, and desperate. Indeed, he's all alone in the world (system), and that's a good thing for the powers that be. All they have to do is clean him up a bit, get him a better suit and haircut, some better shoes, you know, make him *look* the part. Yes, Thaddeus Murfee will be easy to mold.

WHAT WILL A MAN GIVE IN EXCHANGE FOR HIS SOUL?

The position in question is a job as a lawyer in the U.S. Attorney's office, but Thaddeus Murfee will have to crawl before he walks - in so many words. Harold Stuttermeyer explains the duties of the shadowy position to Thaddeus, making it all sound too good to be true. And while he's interested in the position, the young lawyer is also suspicious. He has questions, sure, and Mr. Stuttermeyer has the answers to those questions. Of course, however, there will be a slight probation period. And Thaddeus will be required to pass it. It's all public service, right? Or is it?

Destitute, Thaddeus Murfee can only think of what his salary will be. And he doesn't hesitate to ask. By now, it's crucial if he and his equally meager roommates—including Bud and Winnie—want to avoid being evicted from their humble abode. Thaddeus makes this known to his interviewers, and Mr. Stuttermeyer asks him if he can start the new job on Monday - also offering to float the young, desperate attorney a loan himself to carry him along until his first payday. The offer of one-hundred-forty-five thousand dollars per annum – with all federal benefits - is too good to turn down, and Thaddeus Murfee eagerly accepts it. With that, Thaddeus Murfee becomes a new hire in the U.S. Attorney's office.

All they need to do now is get his fingerprints and mugshot, among other things. Thaddeus understands. And with three little spoken words, the young esquire seals his fate: *I'm all yours.*

WHO DA MAN?

His roomie and true friend, Bud Evans, always told him not to take any crap off anybody. And heeding that advice is exactly what Thaddeus intends to do – no matter what. But is he really as courageous as he wants to believe himself to be? The mannish Melissa McGrant will be the judge of *that*.

YOU GOT SOMETHIN' TO HIDE?

One-hundred-forty-five thousand dollars per annum is a lot of money paid to be the eyes and ears in the U.S. Attorney's office for the District of Columbia. But that's exactly what Thaddeus Murfee was hired to be – the eyes and ears in the U.S. Attorney's office for the District of Columbia. Thaddeus now knows this because the mysterious Melissa McGrant, the woman to whom he will answer during his employment, has told him as much. Rather than practicing law, Thaddeus Murfee will be required to play spy. And the target on whom his secretive superiors have their eyes? Franklin J. Broyles, the U.S. Attorney.

Thaddeus has been given the job of Appointments Secretary. That means he must report back to McGrant *everything* he sees and hears happening with Franklin J. Broyles. If successful, there will be absolutely nothing, nothing at all, that Thaddeus won't be able to have: a lucrative job in any leading law firm of his choice, position options with the FBI, CIA, and NSA, military commissions, coveted bonuses, you

25

name it. But, and that's a great big ol' *but*, he has to be successful in the mission.

All he has to do is be a government spy and gather intelligence on the U.S. Attorney? All he has to do is be their eyes and ears? That's all? Hey, it should be a breeze, right? Yeah, it seems wrong, but who will know besides him and them? They'll protect him, won't they? Won't they? They won't let him fall, will they? *Will they?*

ALWAYS READ THE FINE PRINT.

After giving it some serious thought, Thaddeus changes his mind, he doesn't want the job after all. But it's too late to turn back now, he already accepted it. Plus, he knows too much. He's not going anywhere, literally, if he doesn't complete his traitorous duties. He'll be blackballed with every bar association in America, he will never work as a lawyer. And he'll also be prosecuted – *for something*. Melissa McGrant makes him aware of all the harsh cons, in no uncertain terms. Thaddeus Murfee is not going anywhere, because Thaddeus Murfee was a desperate man. And in his desperation, he made his bones with a group of people he didn't quite understand.

I'm all yours. Three little weighty words that will soon come back to haunt Thaddeus Murfee, Esquire.

FRIENDS AND FOES.

Expensive new suits, French cuisine, only the finest coffee... It's all simply too good to be sinister. In fact, Thaddeus takes an honest liking to Franklin J. Broyles and vice versa. The two men share many things in common and their newfound working relationship blossoms remarkably. No one knows this better than Thaddeus's employers, who manage to know about *everything* going on at all times: what he eats and drinks, how he eats and drinks whatever it is he just so happens to be eating and drinking, etc. Nothing escapes the powers that be. Nothing. This may not go over well with our leading man, but he has no say in the matter. They own him now, body and soul.

THE CHINESE CONNECTION.

Long considered a rival by the American government—at least where it pertains to highly sensitive intelligence—China, or rather its human representatives, makes an entry on these pages in the form of two very untrustworthy individuals: Sing Di Hoa, an MSS agent to whom U.S. Attorney Franklin J. Broyles has questionable ties, and Longma Kee, the menacing Director of the MSS and Sing Di Hoa's boss. These two men are on a global mission. But what is it they want? And what dealings do they have with the U.S. Attorney?

Well, that's for them to know and Thaddeus Murfee, the planted—and expendable—spy to find out. But it won't be an easy task. In fact, it will get downright bloody, vicious, murderous...and ruthless. A price too high for one-hundred-forty-five thousand per annum to cover.

A HIGH-OCTANE LEGAL THRILLER.

Co-starring a relatively small, but powerful, cast of supporting players, including Nikki Broyles, a pre-law student at Harvard, the brainy and beautiful daughter of Franklin J. and Jeanette Broyles, and a sparkle in the eye of our leading man, Jeanette Broyles, the sheltered and pampered wife of Franklin J. Broyles, John Henry "Fitz" Fitzhugh, a high-powered Washington attorney whose top-dollar services Thaddeus seeks out, and LaDonna Smits, Thaddeus's plump and foul-mouthed secretary, this exceptional tale of legal suspense read like classic Grisham during *The Firm* era. I loved this legal thriller and was loath to conclude it. But as the old saying goes, "All good things must come to an end."

Also starring Donald Zang, Freda Jefferson, Evelyn Sunderburg, and Carlos Estancia, who portray a team of well-trained prosecuting attorneys assigned to Thaddeus Murfee, and Tom Behringer and Elizabeth L. Robertson, who both portray high-powered and highly compensated defense attorneys, *Thaddeus Murfee (Thaddeus Murfee Legal Thrillers #0)* is a phenomenal introduction to the fictional works of its authorship, and I'm already in love with the witty and razor-sharp protagonist. Great job, John Ellsworth.

MY HIGHEST RECOMMENDATION.

I loved *Thaddeus Murfee (Thaddeus Murfee Legal Thrillers #0)* and I don't doubt that any true fan of legal thrillers will as well; therefore, I highly recommend it. With that, I'm looking forward to *The Defendants* (Book 2 in the Thaddeus Murfee series) as my momentum is now going at full speed.

Five traitorous stars.

Cat Ellington's Review of The Stepmother by Claire Seeber

My rating: 3 out of 5 stars

Date read: August 2016

THE CINDERELLA EFFECT.

Jeanie Randall, our leading lady, is an English teacher and a single mother with a troubled past. A somewhat neurotic woman who hails from the English town of Brighton, Jeanie—with her only child, a son named Frankie, in tow—is about to start her entire life over, this time for the better, or so she hopes. After a very bitter divorce from her first husband and Frankie's father, Simon, Jeanie is on the verge of remarrying. And hubby number two—Matthew King, respectively—promises to be the Prince Charming she had always dreamt about.

The breathtaking Malum House in Hertfordshire, built atop an old apple orchard in the seventeenth century, is set to be their new home. And the extremely wealthy Matthew is, of course, the ultimate provider. Indeed, he adores Jeanie, and even exchanges pleasantries with the eighteen-year-old Frankie, although their conversations can be awkward at times. Matthew just wants to merge them all into one big happy family, but it's going to be a task. Matthew also has children, two to be exact, who partially live with him in the sprawling manor: fourteen-year-old fraternal twins, Scarlett and Luke. While the two youngsters have their own quarters at Malun House, their joint custody is shared between their father and mother, the blond and leggy Kaye – who is cast here to be a bloody thorn in the side of her successor, Jeanie.

Jeanie is certain about Matthew's love for her. And although hatred and jealousy peer in her direction, she is determined to live happily ever after, such as is fitting for a "princess."

A STRANGER IN HER OWN HOME.

Jeanie is a man-pleaser to a fault, trying so hard to be liked, loved even, by those who harbor resentment towards her, namely her new stepdaughter and her new husband's ex-wife. The males in the family unit don't seem to have a problem with the new woman of the house, but the females? Well, that's a whole nother story. And both Kaye, the scorned ex, and Scarlett, the resentful stepdaughter, have set out to make Jeanie's adjustment into her new life with Matthew a living hell. It shouldn't be this challenging, but unfortunately, it is. The new Mrs. King is walking on eggshells in her own home. But is it really *her* home? Or is it only Matthew's? Why does she feel so uneasy behind the high walls of Malum House? Why can't she seem to fit in? Can Matthew's rich and wealthy friends and associates detect her commonality? Does she really belong here, in their company?

WHO'S OUT TO GET ME?

Everyone has a past. And that would include Jeanie. Her past is marred with imperfections, and not content to just leave well enough alone, it has decided to seek her out. Jeanie knows this because it has reacquainted itself with her by way of mail. Coming back to haunt her in the form of fearful photos mailed to her new, posh residence in stamped envelopes, Jeanie's past threatens to destroy both her present and future. She should tell Matthew, but how can she? And when should she? Will he still love after he learns the truth?

Will she lose her new lifestyle in the wake of it being exposed? She thought she'd escaped those hideous years, but apparently, she hasn't. Who has it in for her? Who's sending the macabre photographs? Who knows her darkest secrets? How did her past learn of her whereabouts? Why won't they forget about her and allow her to move on? And what are those strange noises emitting from the old, stone walls inside of the great Malum House?

YOUR PUMPKIN COACH IS MY PLAIN OL' PUMPKIN.

Nevermind that she snagged the prince, Jeanie is still laden with low self-esteem where it concerns her predecessor, the beautiful, albeit malicious, Kaye. And she's worrying her head damn near gray about the latter. So busy is Jeanie comparing herself to the woman who bore Matthew's twin children, though her sculpted body defies any evidence of it, that she can barely serve as a good (new) wife to him. It's all Kaye this and Kaye that. And it doesn't help when Kaye comes prancing around just to show her successor, who just so happens to also be her "lesser," how much better and prettier she is as a woman. But then again, any woman can look the way Kaye does if she is willing to pay the hefty surgical fees. Worse is the fruit of Kaye's womb, the acidic Scarlett. Like mother, like daughter. What they wouldn't give to get rid of Jeanie.

They can only hope while trying to make her life with Matthew that much harder.

Regardless of her surgically enhanced 'good looks,' Kaye is internally bloated with envy of Jeanie, and the same can be said for Scarlett. For they both want what Jeanie has: the unconditional love and attention of the prince, Matthew. In fact, they'd do just about *anything* to acquire his affections, even if it means ruining the lives of everyone around them, especially Jeanie's. But they're not the only ones who want to destroy her. Someone from Jeanie's past is intent on not seeing her live happily ever after. And if that someone has to expose her for who she truly is to fulfill their heart's desire of hateful revenge, then they most certainly will.

They'll destroy her—and her fabulous new life—if it's the last thing they do.

THE BRITISH ENSEMBLE.

Co-starring alongside our leading lady on the cold and dreary pages of this UK-based mystery thriller is a company of players who contribute passable, not outstanding, but passable performances, including the following:

- Marlena, Jeanie's younger sister, a woman quite odd to say the least, and Jeanie's co-narrator in the world of this tale.

- Alison Day, Luke and Scarlett's godmother, and a very pretentious friend of Matthew and Kay's who seems to find the new Mrs. Matthew King, Jeanie, repulsive.

- Sean Day, Alison's wiry and distant husband, and Matthew's squash buddy and attorney.

- Jill, Jeanie's longtime friend, a former teacher, and a Londoner with a trace of bitterness towards men, especially towards the ones she can't have.

- Miss Turnbull, a gardening neighbor of the Kings, a nosy busybody, and a woman too miserable to have been given a first name.

- Simon, Jeanie's deadbeat ex-husband, and a thorn in the tender side of her luxurious new life with Matthew.

THE LACKLUSTER VERDICT.

I will at least give the author of this tale an A for effort. Though Seeber meant well in her plot approach and produced a decent enough story, I personally found absolutely nothing 'gripping' or 'suspenseful' about this novel. And I am nothing if not finicky where it concerns the psychological thriller genre.

I only finished this book because I don't fancy leaving anything that I start unfinished. And besides, the story wasn't *so* awful that it commanded me to just drop it; however, it was rather 'annoying' in both character performance and pace; and I kept waiting to be 'gripped,' but that edge-of-your-seat feeling never came.

To some readers, *The Stepmother* may be just what the doctor ordered for their suspense fix, but for me, it just didn't penetrate my psyche that deeply. It was decent in its own right, but not once did I ever have to stop reading just to say, 'Oh, my God! This book is just too damned good!'

Again, an A to the author for effort. Because *The Stepmother* is not a horrendous read, it's just not an out-of-the-gate page-turner. The plot simply took too long to unfold. And when it finally did, it didn't blow me away.
I would still recommend The Stepmother to my fellow readers because, you know, what may not be my cup of Earl Grey just may turn out to be theirs.

Happy reading!

Cat Ellington's Review of Last Call by Sean Costello

My rating: 5 out of 5 stars

Date read: September 2016

GNASHING WITH THEIR TEETH.

The fictitious Bobcat, otherwise known as 'The Dentist,' is one reminiscent of Ted Bundy, Jeffrey Dahmer, Leatherface, John Wayne Gacy, and many others of his—real-life—like.

Hunting his unsuspecting prey along the long stretch of one singular Canadian Highway, Bobcat, a petrifying and unrelenting serial killer has a spine-chilling penchant for teeth, and often refers to his unfortunate—and preferably female—victims as 'toads.'

Not a work of fiction recommended for those easily swooned, *Last Call*—a mind-altering tale of unbelievable depravity—claws at and obliterates the reader's resolve, delivering blow after maniacal blow of sheer panic and extreme fright, as only one would come to expect from the tale's adroit creator, Sean Costello.

Scandalous in his afflicted horrors on a myriad of gullible victims, Bobcat runs the bloodstream ice-cold and leaves an everlasting impression on the psyche. And while submerged in the depths of this enrapturing psychological horror, I don't presume that any given reader will find it challenging to commiserate with the quarries of this terrifying madman, knowing that either one of them could be their mother, their sister, their daughter … or even them.

Starring Trish West, a beautiful twenty-year-old leading lady with whom the reader will fall madly in love, *Last Call* is a genuinely impressive script in the field of literature. Sean Costello expertly captures the horrifying nature of Satan's workings within a human host in a way that few authors can in this bone-chilling thriller. And no sooner than concluding it, I could only utter the following words: 'Lord, have mercy.' Indeed, in the wake of concluding this petrifying narrative, I don't think that I will ever look at a camper, or even at a dentist, in the same way again.

Five eerie and dreary stars.

Chapter 2
Mayhem

Cat Ellington's Review of Tourist Season by Carl Hiaasen

My rating: 5 out of 5 stars

Date read: September 2016

FUN, FELLOWSHIP, AND THE MASONIC PRINCIPLES OF BROTHERLY LOVE.

Carl Hiaasen, the great Master of the Crime Caper, does it again with the release of this hilarious gut-buster - straight out of South Florida.

As the curtains open to introduce the author's cast, we make the acquaintance of Mr. Theodore Bellamy (a real-estate man and a loyal Shriner) and his wife, Nell. The couple—who reside in Evanston, Illinois—are on their second honeymoon in Miami Beach, the town chosen by the Shriners International fraternity to hold its huge convention. And, courtesy of his beloved brothers, Theodore and Nell have been provided with only the finest accommodations at the Holiday Inn. It's all good, and the Bellamys are going to enjoy themselves – especially Theodore, who plans to get wasted and hang out with his buddies in a local strip club until the wee hours. Unfortunately, it would be Theodore Bellamy's last hurrah in the three-dimensional physical realm.

MEN-OF-WAR.

After only a few hours of sleep, Theodore is awakened by his giddy wife, Nell, who wants to go swimming. And that, they do. The day is simply gorgeous, the sun is shining, and the breeze is typical of Florida: hot. Nell urges her adoring husband to go in the water first, to test its temperature; she just wants to make sure that it's warm enough for her to get into. And content to please his faithful wife, Theodore Bellamy, a loyal Shriner beloved by all who know him, goes into the sparkling, warm water only to realize that it's full of Portuguese men-of-war. That's right, *poisonous* floating jellyfish. And no sooner does Theodore get into the water than they attack his body, leaving him thrashing out of the surf covered in nasty red welts. It's then that a desperate Nell summons help. Two lifeguards arrive on the scene with a first-aid kit, but the two men are hardly your typical, average-looking lifeguards – at least not according to Nell Bellamy. The two men who arrive to care for her husband aren't the Blond, *Baywatch* types at all. One of the men is African American, and the other one barely speaks English, but Nell is a beggar at the moment. And beggars can't be choosy. Besides, they're wearing lifeguard shirts. The two men inform Nell that they're going to transport her husband, the injured but audible Theodore, to the first-aid station for care, and that she should stay put and await word from the station. Against her better judgment, Nell heeds their advice. But perhaps she should not have, because it would be the last time she saw her husband alive.

"SPARKY," WHERE ARE YOU!

While the South Florida P.D. doesn't seem at all interested in helping to locate the missing person who is Theodore Bellamy (by now, his wife has reported him missing), they are obviously preoccupied with finding out the whereabouts of one D.B. "Sparky" Harper, a famous and very important citizen of the Sunshine State who neglected to show up to work for the first time in over two decades. The boys (and girls) in blue are out in droves searching high and low for the notable "Sparky," but none are concerned with the mysterious disappearance of the lowly Theo Bellamy; therefore, Nell takes it upon herself to enlist the help of the Brotherhood of the Shriners. Indeed, Theodore Bellamy's fez-wearing frat brothers will get to the bottom of it. Or will they?

NOT LIVING OUT OF A SUITCASE.

The fervent search for "Sparky" Harper ends when, while water skiing, a teenager collides with a half-submerged suitcase floating in the water. Believing the case to contain illegal contraband, such as smuggled drugs or dirty money, the teen and his boat-operating friends do a U-turn to go back and retrieve the floating suitcase. And it's when they open it that they make a gruesome discovery: the folded—and amputated—remains of the famous D.B. "Sparky" Harper.

THE ASSASSINATION OF A PRESIDENT.

The revered and endeared president of the Greater Miami Chamber of Commerce, who, of course, had been Sparky Harper, departed from the land of the living on a full stomach, its contents including stone crabs and Pouilly Fuisse. Doctor Joe Allen, the chief medical examiner performing Sparky's autopsy, has just confirmed as much to the investigating officers. Missing both of its short legs, the body of Sparky Harper is now on full display for all present in the examination room to view, but the questions, at least for now, remain unanswered: Who murdered the popular Chamber president? And why? The investigation into his brutal murder now begins. And it will be scandalous, to say the least.

INTRODUCING THE PLAYERS:

- Ricky Bloodworth — When you're hot, you're hot. And in Southern Florida, that expression applies in more ways than one. The mystery surrounding the sudden death, er, murder, of Sparky Harper has become the scorching topic of discussion among the higher-ups. And no one better to turn up the heat on the investigation than Ricky Bloodworth, a wiry, ambitious, and detested reporter for the Miami Sun. Bloodworth is determined to be somebody, and this latest case just may be the push he needs. But he'll have to get through his competitive enemy, Skip Wiley, first. And if Skip Wiley has his way, Ricky Bloodworth will barely scratch the surface.

- Skip Wiley — At thirty-seven years of age, Skip Wiley, a man tanned practically to death, writes a daily column for the *Miami Sun*, and is considered the most famous journalist in Miami. Regardless of his great writing ability, Skip Wiley is a man who's constantly on edge, a ticking time bomb, if you will. A man once approachable by his younger colleagues, Skip Wiley now terrifies them to the extent of total avoidance. And it's just as well as the demons that lurk within the soul of Skip Wiley are beginning to stir.

- Brian Keyes — Tall and blue-eyed with boyish good looks, Brian Keyes is a former reporter for the *Miami Sun* and a brand-spankin' new, albeit underrated and somewhat shunned, private investigator. Because the money he stood to make in the private eye business was simply too tempting to pass up, Brian Keyes says adios to the depressing newspaper business and hello to another branch of investigating. Now on the case of whodunit, his latest workload pertains to the extinguished life of D.B. "Sparky" Harper. Who murdered Sparky Harper and hacked up his body? That is exactly what our leading man is going to find out. But not without some serious consequences, of course.

- Ernesto "No-way Jose" Cabal — A U.S. citizen for sixteen years, Ernesto is still perfecting the English language, not to mention sitting in a jail cell awaiting arraignment on murder charges. Ernesto Cabal is suspect number one in the murder of Sparky Harper, but he insists he didn't do it. Speaking in broken English, Ernesto "No-way Jose" Cabal pleads his innocence to Brian Keyes. Did he do it? Or didn't he?

- Al Garcia — A homicide detective at Metro-Dade police headquarters, and an old buddy of Brian Keyes. Though he talks too much and borders on being just a little too needy, Al Garcia is a good person, and he means well. Brian Keyes may not think that Al owes him anything, but Al surely does. And it's for this reason that Al Garcia will assist Brian with his investigation into the mysterious death of Sparky Harper. Mysterious because the dismembered body of the beloved president of the Miami Chamber of Commerce was not only found in a suitcase but slathered with suntan oil and dressed in weird clothes. Added to the riddle, Sparky had a toy alligator stuffed down his throat.

- Cab Mulcahy — The managing editor at the *Miami Sun*, and a man whose resolve has been completely hardened by his entire adult life in the newspaper business. While Cab is a caring man to a point, it would not be well with one to press his or her luck with him, least of all Skip Wiley. Cab Mulcahy only asks for one thing, and that is for Skip to report the facts, not fiction. But does Skip Wiley (of all journalists) care to respect the wishes of his admirably patient superior? No, of course not. What for? Report what sells newspapers - be it true or not. That's the philosophy of the willful (and very rebellious) Skip Wiley.

- Daniel "Viceroy" Wilson — The former star fullback for the Miami Dolphins who somehow plays a major role in this mind-boggling murder mystery. All broken up and bankrupt, Viceroy Wilson, a has-been who couldn't afford to buy a place in the Football Hall of Fame, even if the League did charge for it, has thrown up his damaged hands and fallen in with a questionable crowd.

- Jenna — Skip Wiley's live-in girlfriend, and the blonde, melon-breasted fantasy girl of Cab Mulcahy.

- Kara Lynn Shivers — A sophomore at the University of Miami, and a tall, blonde beauty queen who soon finds herself caught up in the maniacal chaos surrounding the star players.

- Jesus Bernal — Dubbed the "Defense Minister of El Fuego, Comandante, Las Noches de Dicembre" by his spiritual kin, Bernal is a true believer in the Revolution, and he will do *anything* to defend its mission.

- Renee LeVoux — A twenty-four-year-old tourist from the Great White North (Montreal, Quebec, Canada, to be more specific) who travels to sunny Florida for a peaceful and quiet vacation only to fall into the grubby mitts of one Jesus Bernal.

- Burt and James — Two very loyal Shriners who team up with Nell Bellamy and Brian Keyes to assist in their makeshift investigation into the mysterious disappearance of Nell's husband and their fellow brother, Theodore.

- Ida Kimmelman — A retired widow on Social Security, the extravagant golden girl now lives in a South Florida condo with her fancy little dog, Skeeter. Ida, who only recently lost her husband, Lou, hates the heat of Florida and longs to return home to her cooler, Northern roots; but will she get out in time? Not if a band of dangerous—and murderous—radicals has a say in the matter.

Along with a small set of key bit players, this star-studded cast brings the house that Carl Hiaasen built down with one gut-busting performance after another. And that's not at all surprising considering what has come to be expected of the legendary author. Hiaasen is indeed the master of the crime caper, and here, he once again defends that remarkable title.

A BRIEF SUMMARY.

Someone in Miami is out terrorizing both the tourist and non-native alike. But who can that someone be? Why does he or she have it in for those who only want to come to Florida to visit the Miami Seaquarium, or soak up the sun on the beach, or take in a Greyhound race or a Jai Alai match? What the heck is going on? And whatever happened to the Shriners' very own Theodore Bellamy? The answers are sure to shock the readers of this hilarious tale loaded with mayhem, radicalism, revenge, vindictiveness, envy, and plenty of hungry crocodiles in the Everglades.

Yes, on these wacky pages, the action keeps the reader on edge from beginning to end, and does its authorship fine justice in terms of plot detail, character development, setting, and a great script. And it only further proves why I love the fictional works of Carl Hiaasen on the level that I do.

A FEW FINAL WORDS.

A fun—and funny—read indeed, *Tourist Season* is an effort that I would highly recommend to anyone who has a passion for well-written crime capers, especially those composed by the dexterous hand of the inimitable Carl Hiaasen.

Five sightseeing stars.

Cat Ellington's Review of Behind Closed Doors by B.A. Paris

My rating: 5 out of 5 stars

Date read: September 2016

PREY RIPE FOR THE TAKING.

The incredibly rich and handsome Jack Angel is a man who has it all: money, prestige, respect, admiration, high status in society, and a beautiful wife in Grace. But everything that appears to be well put together on the surface is anything but underneath.

Jack Angel (a successful attorney) and Grace Harrington (a buyer and artist) meet at an outdoor concert on a lush park lawn. The day is as beautiful as the music emanating from the concert stage; and Grace, along with her younger sister Millie (who has the cognitive disability, Downs Syndrome), are out together enjoying the wonderful life they both share. Grace loves Millie, and Millie loves Grace. They have one another, and so far they've done alright. But there's always a chance that they can do better. No one knows this more than Old Scratch, who sends an evildoer—who just so happens to be named Angel—right into their loving midst, to lure them astray with false hope. For the man named Jack Angel comes disguised as a sheep, but there, in the depths of his acidic soul, lies a ravenous wolf.

PROMISES, PROMISES.

By the time their detailed conversation ends, Grace is completely swept off of her feet. And Millie, who dances on the lawn along to the music, is oblivious to it all, caught up in her own vivid world. However, she's not so caught up that she can't see reality right in front of her. And this is it:

Jack Angel looks like George Clooney ('Jorj Koony' to Millie), and he's making her big sister Grace smile. A lover of Agatha Christie mystery novels, Millie smiles when Grace smiles. And the man who looks like George Clooney has just won Grace's heart. Millie watches as Grace dances with him.

Jack has promised Grace the world. And he's even offered to bring Millie along on the journey to a wonderful life. But little do Grace and Millie know, life with Jack Angel will be anything but wonderful. In fact, it will be Grace's worst nightmare.

CONTROL FREAK.

After their magnificent wedding, Grace is settling into her new life with Jack. A magnificently successful attorney, Jack Angel can afford to give Grace the life many women dream of; and because of her new status in society, Grace has become the envy of others, including the tall, blonde, and lithe Esther who, for some odd reason or other, views Grace as a threat to her own existence. Yes, the privileged life of Jack and Grace Angel looks good on the outside—at least as far as their friends can perceive—but behind closed doors,

Grace is a woman who has been beaten and tormented into subjection. She has become the perfect slave to the sadistic Jack Angel. And that's just the way he likes it. Jack Angel is in love with his power over Grace, and he revels in her fear of him. Grace needs him for everything, even for meals and fresh air. Even for a piece of chocolate. And with each passing day, the level of hell that Grace has found herself on only gets hotter, more maniacal, torturous, and inhumane. She has counted every second, minute, hour, day, and week of eighteen months. Nevermind having the most spectacular house in the English village of Spring Eaton, Grace counts down every single day of her secret misery. Nevermind the lovely furnishings, the many works of fine art that hang on the walls, and all of the enviable landscape, Grace counts down every second, minute, and hour of each day: for hers is an existence that's anything but enviable. But can she tell that to those who dare to believe otherwise? Absolutely not. Because where the carnal-minded are concerned, the man named Jack Angel can do no wrong.

Oh, how dangerous it is to be foolish … and spiritually blind.

ALSO STARRING...

The rich and wealthy frolic together. And joining our all-star cast on these phenomenal pages of nail-biting suspense are none other than a group of close friends who are so casual (and catered to), that the reader only makes their acquaintance on a first name basis. They are as follows:

- Diane, a lover of good food, fine wine, leisure, and gossip, Diane is an old friend of Jack's, and has often played the matchmaker in his love life.

- Adam, a lucrative attorney, Jack's professional colleague, an avid golfer, a lover of life's greatest pleasures, and an endearing husband to Diane.

- Esther, a woman who is uptight but thorough, a snooty socialite, a classical pianist, a complicated wife to Rufus, and the woman whom Grace is always eager to please and impress.

- Rufus, a powerful attorney and partner in Jack's firm, a keen art lover, a world traveler, a supportive husband to Esther, and the man whom Jack is always eager to please and impress.

- Sabastian and Aisling, the spoiled, privileged, and private school educated children of Rufus and Esther.

- Kate and Emily, two of the dearest friends that Grace had ever known before they soon faded into the dark and murky shadow of Jack Angel.

- Mrs. Goodrich, the kind and understanding headmistress at Millie's private school.

- Janice, a woman of considerable patience who serves as Millie's carer at her private school.

- Giles and Moira, a chipper couple, and close friends of Jack's. It is Giles and Moira who open their spacious and luxurious home to Jack and Grace to hold their opulent wedding.

- Mrs. Johns, a good housekeeper for the Angels.

The preceding cast, however small, packs a very powerful punch on these fast-moving pages, doing this tale of arctic suspense enormous justice! And they are a set that the reader will not soon forget.

PERCEPTIONS AND DECEPTIONS.

From London to New Zealand to holidays in Thailand, the perfect couple—which just so happens to be Jack and Grace Angel—is caught up in a whirlwind of lust, passion, hatred, rage, lies, slavery, and murder. And before the final page unfurls, the reader will be stunned speechless – just as I was.

NOBODY'S PERFECT.

If it sounds, looks, or feels too good to be true, chances are it is. And it would be well for one to run like hell.

Though some of us strive to obtain perfection, well, perfection is simply unobtainable, as we humans are all flawed. Madness, on the other hand, is a completely different matter. And *Behind Closed Doors* exposes the psychologically deranged perfectly. (Gasp!) Did I say that word? *Perfectly*?

B.A. Paris's *Behind Closed Doors* is one exceptional novel! From the first chapter, it comes out of the gate at full speed and doesn't stop until the gut-wrenching end. And I loved it. I loved this book as it is truly creepy and undoubtedly suspenseful.

The plot is perfect (there's that word, *perfect*, again) as the story unfolds in both past and present tense, in the first-person narrative of our protagonist, Grace. And I just couldn't get through the pages of this terrifying tale fast enough. It's almost surreal how the story grips its readers and pulls them into the realm of its characters' lives. I felt as though I were right there in the trenches with Grace and Millie, and found myself thanking God for inquisitive folks like Esther.

If truth be told, I found myself wishing that I could go into the story and bash Jack Angel's skull in. That's how entrenching the storyline is: you'll feel as if you're there, right there in the intense and suspenseful action. And that's saying something.

Behind Closed Doors is an excellent read and worthy of its perfect rating here. Oh dear, that word, *perfect*, again. Never underestimate anyone. *Ever*.

Five *perfect* stars.

Cat Ellington's Review of Live to Tell by Bianca Sloane

My rating: 5 out of 5 stars

Date read: November 2016

THE ORIGINS OF CHARLES AND JILLIAN MORGAN.

Meet Dr. and Mrs. Charles Morgan, the king and queen of Winnetka, a tony North Shore suburb located seventeen miles north of Chicago. When Charles, the blue-blooded product of wealth and old money, met Jillian, it was love at first sight.

In the beginning, when their love had been fresh and new, Charles and Jillian were students at Cambridge. And it was on the warm Autumn day when Jillian asked him if he had a light for her standard Virginia Slim, that Charles Morgan saw cartwheels spinning in her icy blue eyes. The two fell in love. And their future together was to be nothing but bright … and ridiculously prosperous.

That was then. So long ago and so far away.

Now, it's different.

When was it that the scorching spirit of hate entered the body, mind, and soul of Jillian Morgan? When did she suddenly realize that she actually hated her own husband, Charles? When did their love, and their happiness, and their carefree carousings die? When did their marriage bed get cold?

When did the cartwheels stop spinning?

UNHAPPILY MARRIED.

After each long day of dealing with his patients at the hospital (his real home, by the way), in addition to his extracurricular activities, including golf and squash matches, Dr. Charles Morgan, a greatly successful cardiologist, never arrives home to open arms just waiting to hug him close, or kisses, or kind words, no, but to the contrary, Charles, upon his arrival home, is only met with tension, and malice, and scorn, and bitter jabs that all stem from his frosty wife, Jillian. Long gone are the happy days of their honeymooning in Monaco.

By now, Charles and Jillian have become an Atom bomb just waiting to explode, as the atmospheric pressure in their ritzy home has reached a peak level of volatility. And who's fault is it? Charles is a workaholic who spends more time out of the home than within it. And Jillian feels neglected and lonely. The whole day long she sits all alone in an unhappy home. And who's to blame? She's miserable, but Charles doesn't seem to care, or rather prefers not to. There is no compassion, no communication, no understanding...and no empathy. It's just a dead home shielding dead lives. Sure,

Jillian, who holds a degree in Art History could've been one of the best gallery curators in Chicago. Sure, Jillian, with her flair for high fashion could've taken a job at an exclusive Streeterville or Gold Coast boutique, but she didn't. No, she neglected her own career aspirations to appease the Morgan clan, particularly Charles's mother. Jillian neglected her own aspirations to mingle with the well-to-do of Chicago's ultra-riche North Shore. She neglected her own career aspirations to become a stay-at-home *Mom*. And now she's living the most horrible of lives, even that of regret. And she blames Charles. Not herself, but Charles. *Charles* didn't put off his dreams, but she did. *Charles*. *Charles* pursued his dreams. And now that he's on solid ground, professionally, *she* has become neglected. And if there is one woman who hates to be ignored, it's Jillian.

The pressure is building within the posh Winnetka abode of Dr. and Mrs. Charles Morgan. And sooner rather than later, one of them is going to explode.

The pressure builds...

ENTER THE OTHER WOMAN.

In his social circles, Dr. Charles Morgan can still manage a good chuckle here and there while making merry conversation with his professional peers. And he often looks forward to the big medical functions just to have an excuse to escape the glaring and daring eyes of his arctic wife. The night that he meets a lowly waitress named Tamra

Washington is no different. While killing time to keep from going back to his unhappy home, Charles heads into a Michigan Avenue bar for a drink – Scotch, neat. Tamra serves the great doctor his drink, and the two exchange pleasantries, including name introductions. The attraction, particularly on Tamra's part, is immediate, and this is not lost on Charles. She hopes to see him again. And she will – in more ways than one.

In due time, Charles and Tamra embark on a torrid affair. And before long, they venture into the slitty eye line of a certain woman who has, for quite some time now, desired to have the loins of Dr. Charles Morgan all to herself. But rather than choosing to bed her behind Jillian's back, Charles has chosen the intimate embrace of Tamra Washington. And his secret admirer is now livid, pride and ego clawing at her mind: *How dare he give himself to this...this nobody! This...this waitress! You're beautiful, professional, and rich, but he chose her over you?! Some lowly waitress?!*

Yes. A lowly waitress.

And a Black one at that.

Cue the envious drama. Cue the jealous madness. Cue the covetous vengeance.

Cue the act of cold-blooded murder.

AN ENSEMBLE SO DIVINE.

Cast on these undeniably fantastic pages brimming with sublime action, thrills, and suspense, is a first-rate ensemble worthy of the National Book Award, including the following:

- Chase Morgan, a second-year law student, and the eldest child born to Charles and Jillian Morgan. Unlike his younger brother Gabe, Chase is the doppelgänger of his father.

- Gabe Morgan, an 18-year-old Columbia-bound aspiring writer, and the youngest child born to Charles and Jillian Morgan. With his fair coloring and icy blue eyes, young Gabe takes more after his mother.

- Walter Ryan, a tall dark-skinned, and handsome interventional cardiologist, a Northwestern alum, and Charles Morgan's best friend and golf buddy till the end.

- Vanessa Shayne, an internist who specializes in women's heart issues, Charles Morgan's trusted equity partner in their medical practice and a stunning woman who is desired by all men and hated by all women.

- Clayton and Celia Morgan, the so-called grand duke (and duchess) of the North Shore, scions of Chicago society, and the extremely stuck-up and pretentious parents of Charles Morgan.

- Charlotte Morgan, a University of Chicago alumna, CEO of the Morgan family real estate empire, yet another blonde-haired, blue-eyed debutante, and Charles Morgan's kindred spirit and sister.

- Marion Vaughn, the arrogant, unattractive, and mannish mother of one Jillian Morgan.

- Henry Vaughn, a former rower, a retired textile magnate, a scotch drinker, a man's man, and the boisterous father of one Jillian Morgan.

With special appearances by Tina Ryan, who portrays the very tall, stylish, uppity, and privileged wife of Dr. Walter Ryan, C.K. Morgan, who co-stars as the head of the Morgan Family Foundation and Charles Morgan's cousin, and Neil Yancy, who plays his bit part well as the bullish and violent ex-boyfriend of Tamra Washington, this cast, a scandalous set of the haves and the have-nots, is a gifted ensemble worthy of the record books. And I shall never forget them.

UNPRECEDENTED TALENT.

By now, it should be crystal clear that Bianca Sloane is a mightily blessed wordsmith. Once again—as the author's latest effort *Live To Tell* undeniably proves—her fast-paced, nail-biting, and on-the-edge-of-your-seat style of suspense had me enraptured from the first page to the last. And while it's no surprise, considering that Bianca Sloane is the subject about whom I speak, even still, I am compelled to admit that her literary creativity is simply stupendous.

Not inclined to bore its reader, *Live To Tell* solidifies and justifies the greatness of Sloane throughout its entirety, leaving no room for dispute or refute. And no reader—especially not anyone partial to the grade A class of apprehensive fiction—should have his or her library deprived of the powerful narrative.

Legend does not constitute quantity, but, rather, quality. And in the case of Bianca Sloane, the quality of her literary contributions have the potential to stand the test of time.

Live To Tell is Sloane's fifth perturbing tale of suspense – preceded only by four equally regarded 5-star page-turners, including *Killing Me Softly*, *Sweet Little Lies*, *Every Breath You Take*, and *Missing You*. And you should consider it greatly recommended.

Five blonde-haired and blue-eyed stars.

Cat Ellington's Review of Skinny Dip by Carl Hiaasen

My rating: 5 out of 5 stars

Date read: November 2016

LOVE OVERBOARD.

Florida biologist Chaz Perrone and his lovely wife, Joey—a trust fund baby, by the way—are spending their wedding anniversary aboard the luxurious Sun Duchess cruise liner. It's April in Miami, and the Perrone's are all aglow as they prepare to visit some of the most exotic locales in the world, including Puerto Rico, Nassau, and the Bahamas. The Sun Duchess is a lovely vessel indeed, offering round-the-clock buffets and activities for its guests, including rock climbing, tanning parlors, and golf. And the Perrones, especially the gluttonous Chaz, intend to take full advantage of every sumptuous amenity.

They sail.

Joey Perrone—our leading lady, by the way—is looking forward to basking on the cruise line's unspoiled private island, "Rapture Key," which she fell in love with the idea of after reading about it in the glossy brochure. But as it turns out, the so-called unspoiled island actually belonged to a heroin smuggler who was dismembered by his more ruthless competition, and the cruise line had been able to acquire the land at a bargain-basement price.

They sail.

While they're supposed to be cruising aboard the fabulous Sun Duchess in celebration of their wedding anniversary, the Perrones are doing anything but spending quality time together. Chaz just wants to jet ski, rock climb, play golf, eat, and cheat; but Joey, on the other hand, only wants to lay in the shade and read her books. She's hardly enjoying this little getaway, and it shows. Sure, she thinks about having a little fling, but she just can't bring herself to do it. Chaz is an anus, yes, but she just can't lower herself to his level. Good ol' Joey.

They sail.

Things appear to be looking up—where their unhappy marriage is concerned—when a chipper Chaz returns to their cabin to serenade his wife with an invitation to dinner. Joey agrees and they go. Maybe now they can talk. At dinner, they do just that as Chaz makes it his job to top-up Joey's wine glass. Of course, she notices his actions but really thinks nothing of them. Good ol' Joey. Always willing to give someone the benefit of the doubt. But here, she gets caught off guard. Chaz is smiling.

They sail.

Chaz Perrone, as he smiled and continued to top-up his unsuspecting wife's wine glass, had a sinister plan all along. He was going to kill her. He just needed the right moment to do it. He even knew *how* he was going to do it. He just needed to be cool and wait. And while they were having dinner, he gazed at her, smiling and making gleeful conversation and whatnot. Chaz Perrone, the bastard that he is, *knew* what he planned to do. And he sat there playing the role of the attentive husband, knowing all along what he planned on doing. The weather was perfect as far as he was concerned: an overcast evening mingled with drizzle. And that alone would send the tourists scampering inside. He and Joey would have the stern all to themselves. And that's just the way he wanted it, or rather, *planned* it. By now, Joey is full of red wine—four full glasses, to be exact—and Chaz knows she's more than a bit woozy. He figures she won't know what hit her, and he puts his godless plan in motion. Although Chaz hates getting wet, he must do just that to carry out his evil actions.

As Chaz and Joey stand at the stern of the Sun Duchess beneath a starlit sky, Chaz Perrone deliberately drops the key to their stateroom and must crouch down to find it. But it's while he's crouching that the immoral man suddenly grabs his wife by both of her ankles so that he can lift her up and throw her overboard. Caught unawares, Joey flips over the railing so fast that she never makes a sound – literally. Chaz never hears the splash, although it would have been nice.

But then again, it was a long way down to the water.

The brightly-lit Sun Duchess continues to sail. And not one Klaxon makes a sound.

AFTERSHOCKS.

The plan had been to get her tipsy enough to limit her abilities. See, Chaz Regis Perrone *knew* that his wife had been a champion swimmer, the co-captain of her swim team at UCLA. And he had hoped that the fall would cause her to break her legs, or at least knock her unconscious. But neither happened. Yes, the impact tore off her skirt, blouse, panties, wristwatch, and sandals, but Joey was alive. And due to the choppiness of the Gulf Stream water, thanks to a brisk wind blowing in from out of the northeast, she was also completely sober and alert.

As she prepares to swim to shore, Joey can only think to herself, *I married an asshole.* True, she did. But now is not the time to wallow in it, now is the time to survive. And *that* she must do. She just has to make it to shore. And as she tries her best to get ahead of the opposing currents, Joey realizes one thing: she's in the friggin' ocean, not a swimming pool.

Before long, her legs go numb and she gives up the struggle. And were it not for a floating bale of Jamaican marijuana, which served as a life preserver for Joey after she passed out in the water, she would have surely given up the ghost and drowned.

I NEED A HERO.

When Joey comes to, she finds herself in the company of a man named Mick Stranahan (a former investigator and Hiaasen novel legend). She can't see him because her eyes are swollen shut from both the saltwater and jellyfish stings, but she can hear him just fine. And he commences to tell her how he came about finding her. While she initially thought that she had been beating off a shark, Joey soon learns that it was actually a 60-pound bale of weed. Stranahan—the man who rescued her—has not only wrapped her in warm clothes but nourished her with hot tea and soup. And Joey takes an instant liking to him as does he to her. Their conversation carries on with Joey explaining everything that happened to her aboard the Sun Duchess up to the time that Chaz threw her overboard. Initially skeptical, Mick Stranahan—a rebel with many causes—soon comes around to believing the woman's story – crazy as it sounds.

Joey Perrone and Mick Stranahan bond with Mick eventually offering to join Joey in her ruthless mission to get back at that lowdown husband of hers. And boy, will her quest for revenge be riotous, wacky, and brutal – especially after her remaining co-stars become involved.

THE TIES THAT BIND THEM.

Yoked together with our starring leads on the enjoyable pages of this outrageous crime caper, are none other than the following:

- Corbett Wheeler, Joey's older and equally wealthy brother. In the wake of their filthy rich parents' passing, Corbett and Joey Wheeler inherit massive, multimillion-dollar trusts that many are tempted to covet.

- Ricca Spillman, a licensed cosmetologist, a woman who makes way too much noise during sexual relations, and Chaz Perrone's desperate (and needy) mistress.

- Karl Rolvaag, a Minnesota native, a man with a penchant for extra-large pythons, and the no-nonsense Broward County detective on the missing person case involving the presumed dead Joey Perrone.

- Captain Gallo, Rolvaag's superior officer, and a man hard on throwing the book at the criminally inclined.

- Samuel Johnson "Red" Hammernut, a dirty old bastard, and an eel to all humanity. As birds of a feather flock together, so do the likes of Samuel Johnson "Red" Hammernut and Charles Regis "Chaz" Perrone.

- Dottie Babcock, the greedy and unlawful aunt of Corbett Wheeler and Joey Perrone.

- Nellie Shulman, the acting vice president for the Sawgrass Grove Condominium Association, detective Karl Rolvaag's next-door neighbor, and a sour woman who hates both Karl Rolvaag and his pet pythons.

- Earl Edward O'Toole (otherwise known as "Tool"), a former crew boss, a scandalous and vile hitman, a menace to the immigrant, a collector of roadside grave markers, and the big, beefy, and seriously hairy flunkie of "Red" Hammernut.

- Rose Jewell, an herbal tea enthusiast, Joey Perone's best gal pal, and a fortysomething knockout with blonde locks to die for.

- Maureen, a feisty ol' golden girl battling cancer, and the apple of ol' Edward O'Toole's eye.

With bit parts played by Marta (as Chaz's supervisor), Carmen Raguso, as the Perrone's hard-up neighbor, Katie Stranahan, who joins her brother Mick in this caper, Kipper Garth, who co-stars as a shyster bum lawyer and Katie's husband, and a woman named Medea who plays a tinny part as one of Chaz Perrone's booty calls, we have ourselves a bona fide—and downright hilarious—winner in *Skinny Dip*. And I will never forget it.

EXALTING A LITERARY MASTERMIND.

How is it that Hiaasen has such a unique way of creating characters his readers just can't help but end up fostering empathy for, even when those characters are unworthy of our compassion? How *does* he do it? A sheer talent for storytelling, I suppose.

On the wild pages of *Skinny Dip*, Hiaasen does it again. Hilariously funny and a tugger on the heartstrings, this novel, which revolves around the tropical surroundings of South Florida, should be considered highly recommended for the crime caper enthusiast. It also has a beautiful ending that makes it just that much more lovable. I both laughed out loud and cried as it got me right here. And that's saying something.

Skinny Dip, a great tale was there ever one, is worthy of its legendary status, as are all of Carl Hiaasen's masterpieces.

Five retaliatory stars.

Cat Ellington's Review of The Husband by Dean Koontz

My rating: 4 out of 5 stars

Date read: October 2016

TO LOVE, HONOR, AND PROTECT.

Never underestimate the power of the marriage vow.

Mitch Rafferty, a stand-up guy, a true-to-form character, and a faultless law-abiding citizen finds himself stretched to both his mental and physical limits when a small gang of kidnappers abducts his wife—whom Mitch greatly adores—and demands that he pay a two million dollar ransom for her safe return. Two million dollars is a lot of money, indeed. It's also a sum that Mitch Rafferty—a middle-class gardener—doesn't have. So what shall he do?

What would you do if such an evil situation landed upon your doorstep? Who can you call when murderers are watching your every move and listening to your every word?

Well, if you become desperate enough, you'll do whatever it takes to save the one(s) you love. You'll do things you never dreamed you would. You'll become a monster of sorts – just like the 'easy-going' man named Mitch Rafferty.

A WORTHY READ.

The Husband is a very likable effort centered around a strong plot and a talented cast of players. And while it's not one of Koontz's best scripts, it will hold the reader's interest from beginning to end with a respectable dose of heart-pounding suspense and sharp-edged dialogue. Yes, there are certain instances where the performances feel forced, but the pace of the tale continually makes up for those tiny imperfections. Overall, Koontz presents a hard-core world that his myriad of readers will feel as though they're right there in the heart of, and few will emerge from it disappointed. I recommend *The Husband* as a cozy weekend read to those who need a little something to relax with after a long week.

Again, *The Husband*, in my opinion, may not be one of Koontz's best works of fiction—as I am particularly partial to his horror efforts—nevertheless, it is still worth reading. Enjoy.

Chapter 3
Lies and Deceit

Cat Ellington's Review of The Best Friend by Shalini Boland

My rating: 5 out of 5 stars

Date read: December 2016

THE INITIAL PRAISE.

This is one absolutely phenomenal novel! The script is well written, the plot is well rounded, the pace is rapid, and the ensemble is flawless. Drenched in madness and suspense, *The Best Friend* takes on the aura of a feature film in setting and mood, and left me feeling nothing but an undying love for its distinction. Determined to become one of my all-time favorite tales in its respective genre, *The Best Friend* kept me so engrossed, that I effortlessly completed it in two days.

SO MUCH FOR BFFs.

While I initially found myself becoming annoyed with the naïveté and gullibility of our leading lady, Louisa Sullivan, not to mention her husband Jared's ignorance with regard to his wife and her gut instincts about the antagonistic Darcy, I couldn't help but love them. And I couldn't help but feel for them as they slowly became entangled in the black widow's web.

Indeed, Darcy Lane is disturbed. And she wants to sink her venomous fangs into Louisa. But why? What had been Louisa Sullivan's crime? And what history do these two women have?

The wealthy Darcy knows that Louisa—a woman lower on the economic totem pole than herself—can barely keep up with her social circles, yet she still 'befriends' her. Darcy lords her riches and wealth over the lowly Louisa, but she does so subtly. Hers is a lavish lifestyle that she 'invites' the impressionable Louisa to 'share' in, but even still, her offerings drip acid. And the more Louisa consumes, the sicker she gets—even to her stomach.

Louisa would have done well to heed her gut, because one's gut will never fail them. Her gut told her that something was wrong. And her gut was right.

THE FINAL PRAISE.

The Best Friend truly lives up to all of its five-star reviews, including my own. And if you fancy a good psychological thriller, the same is a chilling narrative that will command your interest, even into the wee hours. *The Best Friend*—a must-read for any true fan of its respective genre—is an exceptional work of fiction. And of it, Shalini Boland should be extremely proud.

Five competitive stars.

Cat Ellington's Review of Batman: The Killing Joke, The Deluxe Edition by Alan Moore

My rating: 4 out of 5 stars

Date read: December 2016

A PINCH OF ADMIRATION.

Brian Bolland did a terrific job with the illustrations for this Deluxe Edition. The artwork was the first thing I noticed, and I loved it almost immediately. Phenomenal artwork!

Now to the story itself.

WHAAAT?

The actual dialogue was moving along well until confusion interrupted the program. Once that happened, the narrative pretty much lost its way. It also lost me.

The following questions explain why:

What's with the laughter between the two archenemies, Batman and Joker?

Why does the narrative end so abruptly?

Did the Dark Knight snap? Is he playing a psychological game with Joker to lure the Clown Prince of Crime into a snare before he kills him?

Does Batman really kill Joker?

Why are these two huddled together laughing and talking like old chums?

Unfortunately, there is no explanation for any of the preceding questions. And my only thought upon concluding this effort was, *What the heck just happened?*

IN ALL FAIRNESS.

Yes, there has been much speculation concerning the hasty ending, but overall, *Batman: The Killing Joke, The Deluxe Edition* is a fairly decent story. It's also very dark – which suits the taste of the film noir lover in me just fine.

To put it briefly, I would definitely recommend reading *Batman: The Killing Joke, The Deluxe Edition* if you're looking to pass a quiet hour or so. Because the tale, while fleeting, nevertheless manages to remain fast-paced and passably exciting. And if it was not for a few annoying blemishes on the surface of its body text, I would have gladly adorned the graphic with a perfect rating of five stars.

Have fun with this one, Bat-fans.

Cat Ellington's Review of Scare Me by Richard Jay Parker

My rating: 5 out of 5 stars

Date read: December 2016

MEET POPPY.

As this horrifying tale of suspense draws the reader into its sticky web, we make the acquaintance of a young lady named Poppy, who is seated before the webcam on her laptop preparing to engage in a video call with a young man named Brett Amberson. Somewhat of a sleaze, Brett is sipping a cocktail of cranberry juice and vodka, and using his boyish charm to gain an advantage over the woman seated before him on his PC screen. Poppy is lovely, indeed, with dark hair, chocolate eyes, and full, pouty lips; and Brett is ravenous in his lust for her. He just wants to see her bosom uncovered. He wants to tease her, and tantalize her, and explore her—even if only virtually. And he can just taste her lips, dewy from a fresh coat of cherry ChapStick. They chat further. And Brett continues to pour on the charm, flattering no one but himself. Soon, Poppy asks Brett if he wants to see where she hangs out. Brett really doesn't care, he just wants to get down to the nitty-gritty of strip tease games; but Poppy insists. She lifts up her laptop to reveal her location: a utility room. She then asks Brett if he would like to see more. Brett pretends to be interested as Poppy moves beyond the room into another area. The horny Brett is soon looking at a kitchen, *his family's kitchen*. The girl named Poppy then produces a key to unlock a back lounge. And when the door opens, a perplexed Brett can see his father, mother, and sister sitting up in a row on the couch with their hands covering their eyes. Their stillness tells Brett they're dead. Even before he sees the blood pooled in their laps, their stillness divulges their death. Brett can see that their fingers are stuck to their faces with black tape, and he's now in a panic.

Brett's instincts tell him to run, and he does just that. But when he runs into the terrible Poppy on the staircase outside of his bedroom, his young life literally begins to flash before his eyes. With one jab of Poppy's Taser, a partially nude Brett goes down the stairs head-first. He's still alive but not for much longer, as Poppy descends the stairs intent on ending his misery. She does so quickly with one swipe of her sushi knife. And afterward, she goes for a swim in the dead family's swimming pool.

Mission accomplished.

GOOGLE ME.

Will Frost is the CEO of Ingram International, and a proud husband and father. His wife, Carla, is a corporate attorney, and their daughter, Libby, the pride and joy of her parents, is a young lady coming into her own as she travels abroad and lives with her boyfriend, Luke. The Frost family is quite wealthy and can afford only the finest that money can buy, including their luxurious estate, Easton Grey. And until now, they've lived rather lavishly in their English dwellings, extremely careful for nothing but happy enough. Today isn't unlike any other for Will Frost, except that this day is Carla's and his nineteenth anniversary. And Will has made reservations at the exclusive Crawley Manor, a favorite spa of the two most important women in his life.

Their little girl is all grown up now, but still, Will and Carla (especially Will) can't let her go. She'll always be their baby. Will is none too crazy about Libby's boyfriend, Luke. He has reason to believe that Luke is influencing his only child, and not for the better. Libby is at ease to do whatever Luke tells her to do as her self-esteem is not all there. And this just doesn't sit well with her father, Will. The family makes merry, yes, but there's that hidden tension between them all. And if the great Will Frost only knew that the devil has been allowed to sniff out his trail, he would be content to choose his minuscule 'problems' over what lies ahead for him any day.

The great man is in a deep sleep, dreaming about a crab struggling to escape death by boiling when his phone rings. Coming out of the dream world into reality, he answers it, only to be greeted by a female voice with the following query: 'When did you last google yourself, Mr. Frost?' It's 3:17 a.m. and Will Frost is perplexed. He initially thought the voice belonged to his precious daughter, but after gathering his thoughts, he realizes it didn't. He checks his caller ID and finds that the caller's number was withheld. Maybe it was just a prank. Or was it?

When did you last google yourself, Mr. Frost?

That single question would mark the beginning of the worst nightmare Will Frost has ever had. For the devil has finally caught up to him. And he has come in the form of a young woman with an extremely angry and unrelenting vendetta.

REVENGE IS A DISH BEST SERVED COLD-BLOODED.

Like all people living in the present, Will Frost has a past. And his past was not very pleasant. While he's moved on and forgotten much of it, the past has never forgotten him. And after that strange phone call, during which some woman asked him when he last googled himself, Will Frost must now come to his senses and confront it head-on.

Still troubled by the early morning call, a now curious Will heads into his private study, turns on his computer, gives it a chance to boot up, and then opens Google to search his name. Nothing out of the ordinary, initially, just the same ol', same ol'. Nevertheless, Will continues to scan the search page results. And he soon comes to one that grabs his attention, particularly because its link contains his domain name with three x's indicating three kisses: *Kiss, kiss, kiss.* The woman who phoned him earlier used these words right before she hung up: *Kiss, kiss, kiss.*

Compelled, Will clicks on the link to the site and is shocked to see images of his home come into view after the web page completes its configuration. Interior images of his home were never made public, so how is it that they appear here, on a live website? Who has access to his home security system? How did they gain entry? Easton Grey is his fortress. How is it that someone came to compromise its safety? Will is both confused and aggrieved. Confused because he thought sure that he and Carla installed an airtight security system, and aggrieved because Will, a man notorious with his privacy, now has his private life on display for all the world to see.

Who could be behind this? And what do they want from him? Is it those hideous blokes at Motex Radials? Who could have done this bloody deed?

Will Frost will be dumbfounded to know that there's only *one* person behind it all: an embittered woman out for revenge. A woman whose passion to kill is so repulsively insatiable, that she's about to send Will Frost on an international run for his life.

The Amberson family is already dead (and decaying) in Florida. Now Will must fly the unfriendly skies on a cross-continental mission to prevent the next brutal murder … and then the next … and the next … and the next … and the next.
For Will Frost, time is of the essence. And a cold-hearted murderer has made it her job to stay one step ahead of him. And how is it that she manages to do so? Well, because *she's* the one who commanded him to head out on this wild goose chase in the first place. Indeed, Will must now rip and run –

to save the lives of not only those of his professional associations but also those of his precious (and kidnapped) daughter, Libby ... and her unborn child.

Poppy knows what Will Frost looks like, but Will Frost has no clue what Poppy looks like. She can be seated right behind him on the same flight and he would never know it.

Someone motivated by the demon of revenge? Well, he or she can be ferociously deadly.

AS FOR THE OTHERS...

From the United Kingdom to Florida to Thailand to Penang to Singapore to Maryland to Chicago to Bel Air to Baltimore and back, this grisly introduces a very memorable troupe of supporting players who play their parts magnificently, including the following:

- Luke Chandler, the passive/aggressive—and terribly controlling—boyfriend of the docile—and terribly spoiled—Libby Frost.

- Mr. Taylor, the new security guard at Ingram International.

- Nissa, the tall, stylish, Irish, and highly attentive PA to Will Frost.

- Tam, a six-year-old delivery boy with a vivid imagination, and an angel in disguise.

- Songsuda, Tam's lazy, fast, rebellious, and good-for-nothing older sister.

- Teddy Boy Pope, a fifty-five-year-old has-been of a journalist, seeking renewed fame through his coverage of the Amberson family murders.

- Weaver, Teddy Boy Pope's trusted and long-time cameraman.

- Lenora, a thirty-three-year-old nursing home worker, and Teddy Boy Pope's love interest.

- Patrice Pope, the embittered ex-wife of Teddy Boy Pope. Here, Patrice is graced with a small speaking role.

- Anwar Imam, Ingram International's cross-cultural management consultant, and a close friend of Will and Carla Frost.

- Molly Monro, perhaps the luckiest little girl alive.

- Jacob "Jake" Franks, an Illinois senator, and perhaps the unluckiest middle-aged man that ever lived.

- Wesley Monro, former private secretary to one Richard Strick, and not exactly your average family guy.

- Zhi Ping Ren, a notoriously proud and arrogant man of the medical profession, and prey in the eyes of the Predator.

- Eva Lockwood, the half-Dutch anthropologist with a deep and deadly connection to Will Frost.

THEY WHO ARE THE HUNTED.

Holt Amberson, a successful St. Louis business entrepreneur, Richard Strick, Lieutenant Governor of Maryland, Wesley Monro, Jacob Franks, Dr. Zhi Ping Ren, and, of course, Will Frost are all very rich and prominent men of the world who share one blood-curdling thing in common: they're all being hunted by a young, pale, and frail woman motivated by unforgiving retribution. And in her bony hand is the wicked sushi knife.

APPROACH WITH CAUTION.

For what it's worth, Richard Parker does an excellent job with this menacing tale of ferocious mayhem. *Scare Me* opened just a bit sluggish, but once it got off and running, it got off and running. The plot, however vindictive, is nearly airtight, only allowing for a little breathing room; and the antagonist is a woman who will haunt the reader's nightmares. Indeed, Poppy, an enthusiast of cherry *ChapStick* is not a character intended for the faint of heart.

For two nights in a row, I was up till past 3 a.m. reading. And I will never forget this tale.

Dear reader, *Scare Me* is truly hard to stop once you get started. And its bone-chilling premise is sure to do a number on your psyche.

This horrifying, dark, and suspenseful mystery thriller is one that I would highly recommend to those pundits of the macabre as you won't be disappointed. Very graphic in imagery, *Scare Me* tells the story of just how cold-blooded a murderous rage can be. And I would only advise that you brace yourselves for an up-close look into an utterly dark, cold, hateful, and murderous human soul.
I pray there will be a sequel.

Five blood-shedding stars.

Cat Ellington's Review of Oscar's Night: An Extreme Novella by Matt Shaw

My rating: 5 out of 5 stars

Date read: December 2016

Fanatic

/fəˈnadik/

noun

a person filled with excessive and single-minded zeal, especially for an extreme religious or political cause.

Indeed, this is an extreme novella. It is not so much horror—as it doesn't venture into the supernatural—as it is chilling psychological suspense (think Stephen King's *Misery*), but it was authored by Matt Shaw. And that means you can expect a hearty helping of blood and violence, even as much as you can stand. One should also keep in mind that many of Shaw's books come with advisory warnings: 'If you offend easily, don't buy the books.' He lets us know ahead of time, boys and girls, lest any of us should be faint-hearted

Shall we?

THE BRIEF ANALYSIS.

Oscar's Night is a dark, chilling, and gut-wrenching read. It's very detailed in both graphics and text and will leave quite a

wicked impression on the psyche. It is for a certainty the reader of this eerie novella will gain an entirely new respect for both those who are public figures—particularly those creatives in the entertainment industry—and the various forms of maniacal stalkings that they often find themselves subjected to from obsessed members of the general public who call themselves 'fans.'
On these transient pages, the terrifying spirit of such an individual is the true horror.

Here's some advice, if I may use this opportunity to offer it: Never, ever try to reason, logically, with someone who is mentally disturbed. Because you'll lose. It's a losing battle.

On these perturbed pages, our leading man—pun intended—and the famous supermodels he surrounds himself with, learn that lesson the hard way.

Five camera-ready stars.

Cat Ellington's Review of Titania's Suitor by C.L. Shore

My rating: 1 out of 5 stars

Date read: January 2017

SERIOUSLY?

Did I really just read 228 pages of emailed messages between two women—one of whom happens to be highly neurotic, insecure, and needy as hell—only to have come to such a horrible, pathetic conclusion? Did I really just waste my time here? Yes, unfortunately, I did. This effort is described as a 'suspense thriller,' but a suspense thriller is hardly what it is. In fact, the same, as far as I'm concerned, is a pitiable insult to the subgenre. This novel—if it could even be called one—is by far one of the worst that I have ever had the misfortune of reading. And I have read quite a few in my time.

For hours, even over two-hundred pages, the narrative—which is basically a diary of frustrating email messages between a pair of girlfriends—goes back and forth while haplessly intertwining with a weak, miserable plot, and a pathetic villain. And I am extremely disappointed with this work, to say the least. No sooner had I completed it than I made haste to banish it from my digital library forever.

As an afterthought, it was a miracle that I even finished it at all. But then again, I hate to start something only to not finish it. Nothing irks me more than that.

THANK GOD IT WAS FREE.

I wouldn't advise you to waste your time on this dialogue unless you don't mind reading an entire body text of emotionally-needy email messages.

Leading lady Charlotte and her best friend, Veronica, got on my nerves, and the plot didn't fare much better. While a boring, senseless read overall, *Titania's Suitor* was graced with only one positive trait: it was free of charge. And I thank God for that.

Thank God it was free.

Chapter 4
Criminality

Cat Ellington's Review of The Kind Worth Killing by Peter Swanson

My rating: 5 out of 5 stars

Date read: January 2017

HOW TO GET AWAY WITH MURDER.

'Everyone dies. What difference does it make if a few bad apples get pushed along a little sooner than God intended? And your wife, for example, seems like the kind worth killing.'
—Lily Kintner, potential murderess

The work of fiction currently under review was so pleasing that I was compelled to extract an excerpt from it to precede my analysis.

From the moment I read its synopsis, I knew that *The Kind Worth Killing* was an effort I intended to read. And in due time, I worked my way around to it. Remembering the many enthusiastic responses that I'd received from others in the literary community after announcing my plans to read it, including one reply, in particular, from a fellow author who'd raved that *The Kind Worth Killing* was 'A great book!' I delved into it and found out for myself just how genuine their praise of it had been.

Set in New England (I love New England!), *The Kind Worth Killing*—a premise obviously inspired by the great Alfred Hitchcock's film noir classic, "*Strangers on a Train*"—is a page-turning tale of murder, hatred, rage, anger, revenge, and deceit that will keep the reader on edge from the soundless outset to the deafening conclusion.

Each chapter is narrated in multiple viewpoints provided by every key player except Brad. And our leading lady—who also happens to be our protagonistic villainess—is flawlessly portrayed by the beautiful, flame-haired Lily Kintner. On these ruthless pages, Kintner believes herself to be 'an animal going in for the kill.' And boy, does she ever.

Riveting suspense and chilling revelations will ensnare the reader; and the cessation will no doubt leave the same shouting, 'Oh! It came back! It came back!'

Excellent storytelling!

A LOFTY RECOMMENDATION.

Is there any such thing as a perfect murder? Trust that *The Kind Worth Killing* is the kind worth reading.

Five vindictive stars.

Cat Ellington's Review of The Wicked Girls by Alex Marwood

My rating: 4 out of 5 stars

Date read: January 2017

IF THIS BOOK COULD TALK, IT WOULD'VE SAID...

In the beginning, this book tried. It really did. It tried its best to be good. It strove to be thrilling and suspenseful.
It strove to convince me that it had a good plot. If this book could talk, it would've said to me, 'Dammit! I've got a good plot!' Set in its defiance, this book would have gone on to say, 'Don't judge me yet, good reader. Just give me a chance to prove myself to you. Let me prove to you that I have potential.'

At the central point, this book strove to confirm its claim to me, saying, 'I promise you that I'm great. Just don't give up on me. I'll catch up. I promise. I'll catch up, good reader. Just trust me, eh?'

After some time, this book—riding on the fumes of momentum—would eagerly say, 'On the edge of your seat now, eh, good reader? Ha ha'

Nearing its conclusion, this book was now boasting to me, saying, 'See! I told you I was good! I told you that I had potential! You love me, don't you? Heh, yeah, I knew you would!'

GOOD, IF NOT GREAT.

The Wicked Girls—a very good, if not a great effort by author Alex Marwood—is one you're sure to remember for quite some time after you've concluded it as it has its moments.

Its plot? Good. Its character development? Respectable, although there were a few sketchy parts that could have withstood some fine-tuning. While these flaws are minuscule, they don't withdraw too much away from the story; nevertheless, the book ends with one too many unanswered questions and events, thereby retaining an aura of deficiency.

STILL RECOMMENDED.

Despite a slow start, *The Wicked Girls* gathers steam along the way and presents itself as an enjoyable read. And while it was not one of my best-loved thrillers, I would still recommend it to those other readers who just may admire it more so.

Happy reading, all.

Cat Ellington's Review of Naked: A Memoir by LaShantell Chimeremguo Williams

My rating: 5 out of 5 stars

Date read: January 2017

A GREAT TESTIMONY – REGARDLESS OF TRIAL AND ERROR.

Naked: A Memoir is a beautiful testimony from LaShantell Chimeremguo Williams. And though the enemy—of all mankind—sought to blank out many of the book's pages in my e-reader, I continued to view the body text that appeared, eventually getting the overall gist of the author's powerful witness. And I say God bless her. Because the personal testimony that LaShantell presents to her readers on these pages took a great deal of courage to share. And for that, I commend her.

SPEAKING FROM EXPERIENCE.

Each member in the Body of Christ—called and/or chosen to be a servant of the Most High God—must undergo his or her own personal trials and tribulations as well as public persecutions from Satan in the evil world system. And they must be trained, as soldiers, to rebuke the enemy—in all forms: evil thoughts, evil situations, and evil, worldly-minded people—from their minds, in the name of Jesus.

Again, it took a spiritually-mature level of courage for Ms. Williams (Sister LaShantell, if you will) to have testified about her past-dead life in the way she did on the pages of *Naked: A Memoir*. And once again, I commend that courage.

LET NO ONE PUT ASUNDER.

Despite the evil situation that presented itself, in the form of those missing pages that I spoke about earlier, LaShantell Chimeremguo Williams' testimony in *Naked: A Memoir* is still extremely powerful and well written. And I highly recommend it.
Be blessed in your future service to the King, Sister Williams. Good job.

Five corroborating stars.

Cat Ellington's Review of The Magpies (The Magpies, #1) by Mark Edwards

My rating: 5 out of 5 stars

Date read: January 2017

WISDOM.

You shall love your neighbor as yourself.
—Mark 12:31

Each of us should please our neighbors for their good, to build them up.
—Romans 15:2

Devise not evil against your neighbor, seeing he dwells securely by you.
—Proverbs 3:29

Won't you please, won't you please,
Please won't you be my neighbor?
—Fred Rogers

A PSYCHOLOGICAL GUT PUNCH.

It is written: 'Thou shalt not kill.' But the reader of *The Magpies* will no doubt wish that he or she could do just that.

The Magpies is a gut-wrenching, and I do mean gut-wrenching, psychological masterpiece. It is a heartfelt tale of utter evil, petrifying suspense, and rage-inducing anguish. And it will hit the reader right where it hurts the most: in their hearts and minds.

Surely, as you're reading *The Magpies*, you will be forced to take a number of breaks from it—which will be a challenge as this page-turning thriller is difficult to put down—just to clear your mind and to catch your breath: for *The Magpies* is just that phenomenal of a novel, and not merely one for the faint of heart.

BRACE YOURSELVES.

Set in gorgeous London, *The Magpies* conjures an overwhelming rush of emotions ranging from anger and hatred to malice and revenge to confusion and despair. And it by no means lets up until the final page unfurls. Gifted with a gripping storyline, the effort will make the reader wish that he or she can physically transport themselves into its world and embrace its starring leads, Jamie and Kirsty, a smitten young couple who fall victim to their psychopathic, evil, conniving, and murderous neighbors from Hell.

ONE OF THE GREATEST.

Mark Edwards' *The Magpies* is one of the greatest novels that I've ever read in its respective genre. It is a well-written dialogue directed by a precise vision and produced by an ingenuine spirit. And I loved the talent and poise of every member of its cast.

Short chaptered and rapid in pace, *The Magpies* is guaranteed to have a drastic, bone-chilling, and boggling effect on your psyche. And you should consider it highly recommended.

Five hateful, jealous-hearted, and very unneighborly stars.

Cat Ellington's Review of The Edible Exile by Carl Hiaasen

My rating: 5 out of 5 stars

Date read: February 2017

TAKE A BITE OUT OF THIS.

Perhaps to a certain great white shark, the exile tasted like chicken?
Yes, of course, he did.

Does it really matter that *Esquire* magazine consistently denied the manuscripts of our dearly beloved Carl Hiaasen when our dearly beloved Carl Hiaasen went on to become one of the greatest novelists of all time anyway? No, It doesn't matter one damn bit considering the outcome. Carl Hiaasen and his writings are nothing short of superb. Period.

Despite its fleeting pagination of only twenty, *The Edible Exile* was enjoyable from beginning to end. Yes, the narrative does seem to be much longer, but that is only because it's so detailed.
A recommended work, regardless of its length, *The Edible Exile* would be a perfect read if you had an hour or so to chomp away at. It also features a hefty helping of some of that good old-fashioned Carl Hiaasen humor, which is always a major addition to any novel he writes. And while he is also famous for the wacky characters he creates for his

tales, Carl Hiaasen continues that notable tradition on these pages with one, in particular, named 'Sixto.'

A FEW FINAL WORDS.

Sure it would have been great if *The Edible Exile* was a longer novel, but mind you, the dialogue was a lost manuscript, and this ephemeral presentation was all the great author could recover of it. So when you read those analyses in which the reviewer is whining about *The Edible Exile* being too short, or complaining that he or she has been 'cheated,' be not dismayed. *The Edible Exile* is a great short story, and more than worthy of your time.
Kudos, Mr. Hiaasen!

Five gill-slit stars.

Chapter 5
Destruction

Cat Ellington's Review of Manufacturing Margaret by Jason Werbeloff

My rating: 4 out of 5 stars

Date read: February 2017

TERRIFYING TECHNOLOGY.

Ridley Scott's "*Blade Runner*" meets Steven Spielberg's "*AI*" meets Alex Proyas' "*I, Robot*" meets AMC's "*Humans*" meets Stanley Kubrick's HAL 9000.

Taxi cabs don't have human souls, and neither do computerized machines (or robots) if you will. But in this eerie sci-fi thriller, *Manufacturing Margaret*, that is precisely the case. A droid—with feminine programming—who thinks like a human, talks to herself and reasons with herself like a human, and who has a tremendous obsession with the daytime serial *The Bold and the Beautiful*, malfunctions in the most grotesque fashion.

PRODUCT DEFECTS.

Created as the result of megalomania, the female droid falls in love with her 'Creator,' Jim, whom she, or rather *it*, prefers to believe is *The Bold and the Beautiful* character, 'Rick Forrester.' In fact, the droid believes that *everything* revolves around *The Bold and the Beautiful*. And it, this nameless droid, even knows every episode of the famous soap by its individual number. It also knows every character on the serial by name, reciting them all in tranquil order.

Indeed, the droid has an insatiable obsession. And the malfunctioning robot is going to live happily ever after with the handsome 'Rick Forrester,' whom it assumes Jim to be, even if it has to commit a heinous murder to do so.

PERFECT FOR LOVERS OF SCI-FI THRILLERS.

A short story of surrealism, *Manufacturing Margaret* is an entertaining tale that I would recommend to those readers who enjoy a good sci-fi thriller with a dash of horror. While it's not too heavy on suspense, it still packs a punch in its own right. And I am certain that many sci-fi thriller fans will find themselves enveloped in its dark, futuristic plot.

My four-star rating of Jason Werbeloff's *Manufacturing Margaret* was not given as the result of an intolerable storyline, but because of its low level of suspense, a trait that I don't necessarily fancy sci-fi thrillers being ungenerous with. Apart from that, the narrative unfurls at a rapid pace and remains effectively passable. And I am sure you're going to enjoy it, my fellow book lover.

Happy reading!

Cat Ellington's Review of Gone Girl by Gillian Flynn

My rating: 2 out of 5 stars

Date read: March 2017

DON'T BELIEVE THE HYPE.

Quiz:

Nearly everyone—including media journalists, celebrities, and members of the general public alike—is talking about this supposedly great novel of fiction titled *'Gone Girl,'* a *New York Times Bestseller List* honoree, proclaiming it to be, in the words of one particular critique, 'A Perfect Thriller!' and 'An Incredible Media Satire!'

Now after taking all of this lavish praise into consideration, what do you do?

A) Ignore the masses, dismissing their like-minded salutations of the novel as the typical 'herd mentality.'

B) Check out the novel's film adaptation to come to your own conclusion as to whether or not you'd enjoy the book on which the film is based.

C) Buy the book first and read it for yourself – to find out, firsthand, if it really lives up to all of the worldwide commendations.

My answer was C.

Normally, it wouldn't take me very long to read a novel of over four hundred pages. In fact, I could conclude such a novel in a matter of days. But in the case of this overhyped mammoth, which was authored by Gillian Flynn, respectively, it took me nearly two months to complete it – an indication of just how much I abhorred it.

AMY DUNNE? NOT SO AMAZING.

A pathetic excuse for a leading lady, 'Amy Elliott Dunne' is one of the most self-loathing, insecure, immoral, hateful, spiteful, malicious, ugly-spirited, and attention-starved characters that I've ever had the displeasure of becoming acquainted with. And I couldn't stand her.
While she pretends to be this perfectly confident specimen, she lacks self-esteem, she perspires jealousy, and she lies with a straight face. An instrument of hidden evil, there is absolutely nothing amazing about Amy.
With that, I simply cannot fathom the world's infatuation with her. What is it about this particular character that such a large number of women 'admire' so much? Perhaps it's because 'Amy Dunne' represents something about themselves? Perhaps it's because many women in the world only relate to this character because deep down they wish to

be like her? Perhaps they covet fame, fortune, and the love of the world? I would say it's all of the above.

Catering to such a spirit in society, Ms. Flynn uses the following adjectives to describe her principal character: perfect, rigid, demanding, brilliant, creative, fascinating, rapacious, and a megalomaniac. While not all of those are complimentary, somehow Flynn still manages to depict the crooked Amy as some sort of a saint. And I found that to be quite offensive.

While I admire Gillian Flynn as a writer, I'm disappointed in her vision of the fictional Amy Dunne. The way I see it, Flynn dusted the troubled, sadistic bitch with powdered sugar, and then threw a cherry on top of her for garnish. And that just didn't do for me.

Because I foster nothing more than disdain for Gillian Flynn's *Gone Girl*, I will not analyze it in further detail.

MY PERSONAL OPINION.

This book bored me, and it got on my nerves. This book made me sick to my stomach, and I couldn't wait to finish it: for it left a bad taste in my mouth, something awful. And now that I've finally concluded it, the urge to cleanse my palate is one of great strength. So to remedy the gnawing compulsion, I've carefully selected my next read, one that hasn't been publicly 'exalted' and 'revered' by the masses.

As the old saying goes, 'To each his own.' And though *Gone Girl* had not been one of my most enjoyable reading experiences, that's not to say you won't love it, dear reader; therefore, you should consider it recommended based on that chance.

Happy reading.

Cat Ellington's Review of Scar Tissue by M.C. Domovitch

My rating: 5 out of 5 stars

Date read: March 2017

WORDS OF WISDOM TO LIVE BY.

Surely You set them in slippery places;
You cast them down to destruction.
Oh, how they are brought to desolation, as in a moment!
—Psalms 73:18-19

For whatever a man sows, that he will also reap.
—Galatians 6:7

Since it is a righteous thing with God to repay with
tribulation those who trouble you.
—II Thessalonians 1:6

Vengeance is patient in her waiting;
And victory serves as a fierce rebuke to defeat.
—Cat Ellington

Just for the record, I made up the last epigram for the sake of this review.

A GOOD COMPARISON.

Where, oh where are "Lennie Briscoe," "Rey Curtis," "Ed Green," "Anita Van Buren," "Jack McCoy," and "Abbie Carmichael" when you need 'em?

What an exceptional work of fiction M.C. Domovitch's *Scar Tissue* is! The tale reads like a classic episode of Dick Wolf's *Law & Order*, particularly one of those cutthroat episodes from the legendary era of the 1990s. And I loved it from beginning to end. A few forgivable grammatical errors aside, *Scar Tissue* is both a fascinating novel and a five-star worthy must-read.

Dear reader? Shall we?

WANNA KNOW HOW I GOT THESE SCARS?

Our leading lady Ciara Kelly, a famous fashion model, finds herself at the mercy of a cold-blooded serial killer who abducts the beautiful human mannequin after one of her photo shoots, transports her to a mysterious location in a wooded area, and then goes to work on her face and body with knives and scalpels – not to enhance her already perfect person, no, but for the distinct purpose of scarring it with ugly marks that spell out derogatory words. Miraculously, Ciara escapes her obsessed captor, running through the dark, rainy woods and desperately praying for a way out, only to become the victim of a vehicular collision after she unknowingly—and deliriously—runs out in the middle of the road. Unfortunately, the accident lands her in a coma for weeks, thus bringing a painful end to Ciara's lucrative career as both a fashion runway queen and magazine cover girl, not to mention her love affair with the powerful and super-rich Brent Morgan. Even Ciara's world-renowned agent—after beholding her client's scars during an awkward visit to the hospital—isn't severing their professional contract fast enough. Oh, how quickly it all collapses. Ciara Kelly's entire world is suddenly yanked out from beneath her.

As she emerges from her comatose state with no memory whatsoever of her horrifying ordeal, she does, on the other hand, remember her only living relative: her older—and most beloved—sister Dierdre. At Dierdre's request, Ciara moves in with her after she's released from the hospital. And so excited that Ciara is beginning to regain her memory after some time, Deirdre foolishly leaks the good news. But no sooner does Diedre spread the good news than Ciara once again finds herself on the run for her life from the same cold-blooded murderer—who abducted her before—after he learns of her memory recovery. And this time, Ciara Kelly's obsessed stalker—a functioning demoniac—intends to tear her up for good. This time, he'll make sure she doesn't escape.
Or will he?

VASTLY RECOMMENDED.

Scar Tissue is such an excellent read, that I finished it in less than 72 hours!

Set in New York, Seattle, and Portland, *Scar Tissue*, the first in a series dedicated to the memorable Ciara Kelly, is an on-the-edge-of-your-seat, fast-paced, and exciting thrill ride packed with nail-biting suspense and non-stop action.

On these maniacal pages, you get it all: the scorn of New York's most affluent and wicked, the agents of Satan who operate in the Catholic Church, the society page darlings, the kind and the generous, the clueless, the unsympathetic, the greedy, the conniving, the backstabbing, the lying, the deceiving, the whorish, the boorish, the heaven-sent, and the hellbound. These all collide in one of the best novels in the thriller genre on the market today.

Vastly recommended, *Scar Tissue* is guaranteed to command the reader's attention, even into the wee hours as it had commanded mine. And though I didn't want the story to end, I knew it was inevitable that it would.
While I will miss *Scar Tissue*, I'm looking forward to reading *Seeing Evil*, book 2 in *The Mindsight* series. But until then, I would like to say, Great work, M.C. Domovitch! Your skill is admirable, and your vision is fascinating. Kudos to you.

Five scarred for life stars.

Cat Ellington's Review of Vendetta (Xander King, #0.5) by Bradley Wright

My rating: 5 out of 5 stars

Date read: March 2017

LONG LIVE THE KING.

An action-packed adventure awaits the reader on the fleeting pages of this, the prequel novella in the must-read Xander King series.

It's a snowy Christmas Eve in Lexington, Kentucky as the script opens to introduce the reader to its key players, including our leading man Xander King, a US Special Ops legend; his best friend Kyle Hamilton, a somewhat cocky but likable womanizer; and Sam Harrison, a British MI6 operative, Xander King's partner, and the only other person in the world, besides Kyle, who really knows him. Sam Harrison may be a woman, but she doesn't suffer fools gladly when it comes to her job.

A very wealthy man, Xander King is in the process of hosting Christmas at his opulent mansion situated on a thousand-acre horse farm. And joining Kyle and Sam in attendance are Xander's sister Helen—who's making dinner for everyone—and his beloved niece, Kaley, Helen's daughter. Xander's family and his dearest friends are all here and Christmas should be wonderful – or at least Xander is hoping it will be. While the season is merry, our leading man is secretly being troubled by thoughts of his adoring parents, both of whom were brutally murdered more than ten years ago. Xander tries to get on with his very comfortable life, but still, he can't shake the fact that his parents are gone. Moreover, he can't shake the nagging feeling of failure that nips at him on a daily basis with regard to their untimely deaths. Xander has never been able to track down the monster who murdered his parents. And this bothers him. It bothers him to know that the monster is still out there somewhere. And Xander King has never wanted anything so much as to finally capture the monster. He has never wanted anything so much as to finally face-off with the killer of his parents. This has become an obsession for Xander King. And he will never stop looking for the killer until he finds him … or her.

Truly, Xander King is nothing if not patient.

Xander King elects to enjoy the time spent with his loved ones on this cozy Christmas Eve. After visiting his lavish stables, where he'd gone to check on his Thoroughbred racehorses, including his Kentucky Derby-bound colt, "King's Ransom," Xander returns to his opulent residence to join Kaley in a game of Chutes and Ladders. All is well, and all are happy. Kyle and Sam, who, by the way, just so happen to be involved in a passionate, albeit platonic, love/hate relationship, are even immersed in their usual bickering. Xander knows they secretly like each other, therefore he leaves them to it. It's a joyous Christmas Eve. What more could anyone ask for?

HERE COMES TROUBLE.

Helen is setting the dinner table, Kyle and Sam are bickering about Irish coffee, and Kaley is laughing and dancing when Xander's phone rings. Helen forbids him to answer it, but he does so anyway. His caller ID tells him that the caller is Allison Freeman. Allison Freeman is the district attorney in Lexington. And like Xander, she gets a kick out of bringing down the bad guys. So to what does Xander owe the pleasure of a call from her on Christmas Eve? Charles Bowker. Charles Bowker murdered two families before the authorities caught up with him. And after Allison Freeman got him convicted on all charges and had him transported to the state penitentiary, Charles Bowker would only last behind bars for two months before escaping. Allison tells Xander that Charles Bowker has just killed two prison guards inside, and three more outside, before hopping into a Humvee full of armed men and getting away. Of course, this whole thing with Bowker has nothing to do with Xander, but Allison Freeman is now afraid—and worried—that Charles Bowker, a man with a grudge for sure, is going to come after her. He and his posse have already killed more people since his escape, and this too worries Allison. Three Humvees full of armed men will catch anyone off guard. And Jerry Thompson, the Sheriff of Lexington and Xander King's sole nemesis, is way out of his league – despite his being a former Navy SEAL.

Xander detests Jerry, and the feeling is mutual, but he cares deeply for Allison. And right now, she needs his help. His ex-girlfriend is not only in need but also romantically involved with Jerry Thompson, his lesser. And while his machismo and pride work hard to conceal his true emotions on the surface, underneath it all, the extraordinary Xander King is fuming.

Maybe now he can put his fiery nature to good use. Perhaps now he can show Allison what a real man looks like.

Because everyone who's anyone knows that Jerry Thompson, jealous of Xander King since their Navy SEAL days, is nothing but a wuss in comparison to him.

Finally succumbing to his fierce emotions, Xander King agrees to assist in the manhunt for Charles Bowker. And Sam and Kyle will be right there alongside him.

Of course, there will be other Christmases, but for now, they've got a cold-blooded murderer to catch. And they must catch him before he gets to Allison. Xander King, despite his pride, still has feelings for the sexy DA and he makes it no secret. Xander is deep in thought when Allison interrupts his reverie to tell him about the Humvee that has just pulled into her driveway. Time stops for a moment before all hell suddenly breaks loose. A shocked Xander can only sit and listen as Allison becomes the apparent victim of a violent kidnapping. And he and his butt-kickin' and name-takin' team must now jump into action to save her. But will Xander be able to save her in time? Or will another love of his life be lost forever? Should the latter threaten to prevail, Xander

King will turn the entire state of Kentucky over to fry on both sides.

Indeed, Xander King will get medieval on everyone involved – even on those he never would have suspected.

A SMALL BUT EFFECTIVE ENSEMBLE.

Co-starring in this fleeting action thriller is a small but genuinely memorable ensemble of righteous and unrighteous players that will keep the reader on edge until the turning of the final page, including the following:

- Tony Brancati, a ruthless mob boss, a close associate of Charles Bowker, and a fixer of Kentucky horse races.

- Melanie and Kate, Xander's trusted assistants.

- Jonathan Freeman, Allison's brother, and a man about whom Xander King knows very little.

- Tim Lawson, the SWAT team leader in Lexington overseeing the Allison Freeman kidnapping case, a former Navy man, and a huge fan of Xander King.

A DEADLY COMBINATION.

Fighting crime in Humvees, Hummers, Range Rovers, Escalades, and Mercedes Benz SUVs, Xander King and his female partner, Sam Harrison, are not a double team to be trifled with!

For a dialogue of only 85 pages, Bradley Wright's *Vendetta* is one of the most fun-filled and action-packed novellas that I've ever read. A perfect read to pass a lazy Saturday afternoon, the effort is one that I would greatly recommend, especially to those readers who, like me, foster a passion for the United States Armed Forces.

I can hardly wait to get started on Book 1 of the Xander King Series—to which *Vendetta* serves as the prequel—that being *Whiskey & Roses*.
Wonderful work, Bradley Wright! And I commend you for it.

Five H1-driven stars.

Cat Ellington's Review of Nest by Terry Goodkind

My rating: 4 out of 5 stars

Date read: March 2017

THE BRIEF FOREWORD.

The eye is the lamp of the body. If your vision is clear, your whole body will be full of light.
But if your vision is poor, your whole body will be full of darkness. If then the light within you is darkness, how great is that darkness!
—Matthew 6:22-23

THE PROS.

Nest: A Thriller was my introduction to the written works of Terry Goodkind, an author relatively new to the thriller genre. It had become my understanding, before viewing *Nest*, that while science fiction is Mr. Goodkind's primary genre, he also dabbles in the thriller pool. And I must admit that he presents a satisfactory work with the narrative currently under review.

A gruesome tale, *Nest: A Thriller* stars Kate Bishop, a woman who was born with a remarkable ability: she can identify evil, depraved, ruthless, and barbarous murderers just by looking into their eyes. Although *Nest*, a blood-curdling tale, was there ever one, kept me awake into the wee hours every night until I completed it, the storyline unnecessarily dragged out just a bit too long for my taste. Nevertheless, the plot managed to hold my attention, which is saying something, and I am compelled to congratulate Terry Goodkind on a nice effort.

THE CONS.

Even though this story is set in Chicago, absolutely nothing about it *felt* like Chicago, if that makes any sense. The atmospheric setting of *Nest* did not give me the feeling of being in Chicago. And I would know, considering that the Windy City is my nativity. Save for one particular scene that involved O'Hare International Airport—one of Chicago's greatest landmarks—there had been no mention whatsoever of any other Chicago landmarks, neighborhoods, streets, public transportation systems, parks, establishments, citizens, or otherwise. Not even the city's legendary lakefront received a mention. And *that* is one helluva no-no. His failure to truly capture the city of Chicago, in its essence, had been only one—among many—of Goodkind's offensive bloopers here.

A word to the wise, in my best Chicago slang: If you gon' bring in Chicago, you betta bring it in right or you bet not bring it in at all.

Readers should feel as if they're being transported to the setting place of whatever book it is they just so happen to be reading. But on the pages of Terry Goodkind's *Nest*, the reader will not get a true feel of Chicago. This especially rings true if the reader is already familiar with the city, be he or she a native or a visitor.

GETTING THE FACTS STRAIGHT.

Next, unlike the so-called 'genetic breakdown of humans' that co-star Jack Raines so eloquently describes to our leading lady Kate, to better her understanding of human nature where killing is concerned, the reality is an entirely different matter. For one, Mankind was not inherently murderous. Human beings do not have an 'inborn genetic mandate for killing.' The potential to kill is not a part of our 'genetic makeup' as human beings. It's simply the many desires to do evil that war in our members. And these wicked temptations are sent into our minds by Satan, the enemy of all Mankind.

The Lord God gave Man free will: good or evil. One either chooses to serve the Lord or he or she chooses to serve Satan. And since Satan, the enemy under whose sway the whole world lies, was a murderer from the beginning, well, there you have it. Humans who are tempted to murder other humans are doing the will, or the 'bidding,' if you please, of Satan: for he, and he alone, is the only tempter.

Cain was the first *human* murderer. He had murdered his brother, Abel, because Abel had offered up to God a more pleasing sacrifice than Cain's own: for Abel had offered the Lord his best, unlike his brother, Cain. And upon witnessing

Father God's approval of his brother's offering, the spirit of Satan entered and tempted Cain: envy and jealousy begot anger, then anger begot hatred, then hatred begot rage, then rage begot a murderous spirit. It was a layered demonic attack on the human mind.

Satan had only been allowed to do this because the two brothers' parents, particularly their mother, Eve, was deceived by Satan—whose voice spoke to her from the mouth of the crafty serpent—to disobey a direct commandment from her Creator—the Lord God—during the time of her husband Adam's and her dwelling in the Garden of Eden. When Adam had been tempted to follow the lead of his woman, after her mind had been deceived by Satan, the punishment for their disobedience was death.
On cue with Father God's judgment, Satan now had himself a place in this three-dimensional physical realm. And the Serpent of Old, at war with Mankind since the beginning of time, continues to tempt humans—who are open to his evil lies—to do evil in the sight of the Lord God, even to this day.

The battle was never physical but spiritual.

If one ever loses sight of the truth, he or she will find themselves misled by propagandistic rhetoric. And much of what I read in this novel—in my own opinion—was propagandistic rhetoric.

People should never allow themselves to be deceived by what they see on the surface because to be carnally minded is death. One should know that the spiritual is more important than the physical because the spiritual begat the physical. And to be spiritually minded is life and peace. Always remember that if the spiritual being is in error, then the outcome will be evil and vice versa.

Satan the Devil—who is an evil spirit, not a physical being—tempts humans to sin, period. And one of many sins would include committing murder. Killing is not part of our 'genetic makeup.' We, humans, are not natural born killers, but we were all born into sin because Adam disobeyed the Lord God. Because Adam—being a man—was the head of the woman, God held him accountable.

Satan is allowed to tempt humans to mimic his ungodly nature. And unfortunately, many do not resist him.

THAT SAID…

What Terry Goodkind focused on in *Nest: A Thriller* was the physical. He did not explore the spiritual. And this is where he got tripped up. The natural order is always the spiritual first, then the physical. Spiritual warfare brings about physical chaos in this three-dimensional physical realm. If Satan gets taken out, peace will dwell; but if Satan is allowed to roam in the physical realm, chaos will continue to have a place. And because the Lord God gave Man free will, Satan must be allowed—for an allotted time—to roam in the physical realm and tempt the minds of human beings.

That said, Terry Goodkind still deserves a desirable rating for this literary attainment. *Nest: A Thriller* is not a bad read, but it falls short—pun for fun—in the area of offering up misguided information, not to mention chapters that are not only too long but bloated with a lot of boring and unnecessary information that could have been omitted. Also, the plot, though captivating, took way too long to unfold. And it was a torturous experience taking into account how extended the chapters are.

While the cons may outweigh the pros, Terry Goodkind gave the conclusion of this tale his all. And despite the cons, the pros of such an ending cannot be overlooked. For this reason, I am giving Terry Goodkind's *Nest: A Thriller* a satisfactory rating of four stars. And for those of you who love dark thrillers smothered in chilling suspense—and garnished with plenty of gore for presentation—I would favorably recommend it.

Happy reading, all.

Chapter 6
Falsehoods

Cat Ellington's Review of The Marriage Pact
by Michelle Richmond

My rating: 5 out of 5 stars

Date read: April 2017

A QUOTE.

Marriage is an institution ordained of God and is not to be entered into lightly or in jest and only after much consideration.
—Universal Life Church

GIVEN IN MARRIAGE.

We are gathered together here to unite this man and this woman in the bonds of matrimony.

Do you, Groom, take this woman to be your lawfully wedded wife, to have and to hold, in sickness and in health, in good times and woe, for richer or poorer, keeping yourself solely unto her for as long as you both shall live?
If so, say, "I Do."

Do you (Bride) take this man to be your lawfully wedded husband, to have and to hold, in sickness and in health, in good times and woe, for richer or poorer, keeping yourself solely unto him for as long as you both shall live?
If so, say, "I Do."

Ah, the sanctity of marriage.

LET NO MAN PUT ASUNDER.

While reading the eerie description for Michelle Richmond's *The Marriage Pact*, I felt my sentiments heighten to a great level of excitement. Because I knew that the novel was going to be one that I would find genuinely enjoyable, depending on whether or not it lived up to its heart-pounding chronicle.

Thankfully, it did not fail.

Set in San Francisco, the plot, narrated in the first person by leading man Jake Cassidy, orbits around both he and his new wife, Alice, a pair of newlyweds looking forward to a wonderfully bright future ahead. That is until one of their wedding guests, a former Irish folk music star turned businessman named Finnegan sends the blissful pair a wedding gift destined to change their lives forever. The small gift box that Finnegan gives Jake and Alice is etched with two simple words: *The Pact*. And it would have been better for the newlyweds had they never opened it.

Jake—a very empathetic therapist to both married couples in distress and troubled teens—and his new bride Alice—a former rock star turned attorney who incidentally stands to gain a promotion for partnership at her law firm—initially overlook the gift box, which was delivered to them equipped with two very expensive pens, as simply another one of their many wedding gifts. In fact, a few days would pass before Mr. and Mrs. Jake Cassidy actually got a chance to go through the contents of the fancy box. Instead, they laugh and make light of it all.

After some time, Jake and Alice call Finnegan to thank him—and his wife—for the gift box. And it is during this time that Finnegan replies and provides Jake and Alice with a brief pitch as to what "The Pact" actually is. Jake and Alice—far too naïve for their own good—both agree to a sit down Vivian, a representative from "The Pact," who pretty much schmoozes Jake and Alice with a rehearsed biography about a woman named Orla who founded "The Pact" and runs it from her sprawling estate in Ireland. Orla's philosophy is based on the principles of encouraging strong, healthy, and long term marriages. Notwithstanding, "The Pact" even has its own Manual which includes sections detailing how husband-and-wife members must conduct their everyday activities around each other, and the penalties they stand to face should either one of them fail to do so.

These terrifying penalties are unknown to Jake and Alice because Jake and Alice couldn't be bothered to read the fine print of the so-called Manual, let alone any of its clauses. They should have read the Manual carefully during Vivian's initiation, but they didn't. And because they didn't, Jake and

Alice will soon learn—the hard way—that reading the fine print before signing on the dotted line is never an option, it's a must. When Jake and Alice finally join "The Pact," the gullible newlyweds soon learn that NO ONE escapes "The Pact," at least not alive. And it is here that an embittered regret makes its entry.

MY SUMMATION.

The Marriage Pact will make the reader feel as though he or she has been shoved into a maniacal asylum with the extremely depraved, and left there with absolutely no way out. Indeed, it is a deeply emotional and gut-wrenching roller-coaster ride through the trenches of madness. Everything that you've ever heard about the deranged and demonic beliefs and practices of cults and sects can be summed up in this frightening page-turner. While the members of the "The Pact" all refer to one another as 'Friend,' their evil actions expose them to be anything but.

Short-chaptered and transfixing, Michelle Richmond's *The Marriage Pact* is an arousing narrative that is guaranteed to keep the reader entangled in its lunacy. Expect your emotions to run wild with this dreadful tale as it invokes feelings of frustration, anger, fear, paranoia, anxiety, worry, doubt, and every other sensation in-between.
I didn't know when or where it would end, but in time, it did. And in such a way that will leave the reader in tears and speechless. Most deserving of my five-star rating, *The*

Marriage Pact is a skillfully-written work of excruciating suspense!

MY RECOMMENDATION.

With regard to detailing the blind falsities of cultism, do I, as a professional reviewer, acknowledge Michelle Richmond's latest work of fiction to be one of the most illustrative—and petrifying—accounts that I've ever read? I Do.

Five homewrecking stars.

Cat Ellington's Review of The Address by Fiona Davis

My rating: 5 out of 5 stars

Date read: April 2017

BREEDING. IT'S IN THE BLOOD.

Past and present collide in this well-researched, not to mention well-written, jewel of literary perfection. *The Address* draws the reader into the esteemed sphere of the nineteenth-century Gilded Age with all the aristocratic snobbery and cultured etiquette of a purebred Astor.

I am entirely impressed with this captivating work of historical fiction, and I commend the talents of its respective authorship, Fiona Davis. I loved *The Address* so much that I hated to part ways with the storyline upon reaching its conclusion; but, as they say, 'All good things must come to an end.'

Even though *The Address* is a tale of historical fiction, it is also inspired by any number of actual events, some of which the reader may have never known about until now.

Set in both London and New York, and transcribed in the journalistic style of a diary, *The Address* is a period novel that extends 100 years in sequence—from 1884 to 1985. And the script unveils the lifelines of a family named Camden, which has its wealthy foundation rooted in the work of a famous architect named Theodore "Theo" Camden.

Dear reader? Shall we?

LONDON, 1884.

The breathtaking story commences unfolding when our leading lady, Sara Smythe, head housekeeper at the renowned Langham Hotel, notices a small child wobbling on the window ledge of one of the grande inn's fifth-floor accommodations. Terrified that the female child is in danger of plunging to her death, Sara immediately runs back into the hotel and upstairs to the child's room to coax the little girl back inside while summoning the help of two members of her housekeeping staff. After luring the frightened child back into the room, Sara then meets the girl's beautiful mother, Minnie Camden, an elite socialite of the aristocracy who soon returns to the opulent suite and learns of the near-tragedy that resulted from the family's maid who neglected to mind her post.

Enter Theo Camden, a renowned architect and Minnie's husband, who too receives a briefing on the goings-on concerning his child after he succeeds his wife into the family suite. Theo and Minnie both thank the relieved Sara, and everything returns to normal.

Sometime later, an indebted and charismatic Theo, apprentice to the great Henry Hardenbergh, by the way, invites the lowly Sara to have tea and cake with him to (1) express his gratitude to her for saving his child's life, and (2) offer her a more prominent job position in his native America. Theo Camden assures Sara that she'll be working for him in the *Dakota*, a newly-built, elaborate, and luxurious apartment house that he and his partners are constructing from the ground up. And needless to say, Sara is grateful and excited for the opportunity. *Dakota* is the talk of the town. And unbeknownst to Theo and Sara, it will be the same *Dakota* that would serve as the setting place for the real-life murder of one of the greatest singer-songwriters of all time: John Lennon. Nearly one-hundred years later, the extremely-troubled Mark David Chapman would gun Lennon down outside the ritzy walls of the *Dakota*, heightening its fame.

Mr. Camden's job offer is too good to pass on, therefore, Sara agrees to it.
No longer will she be subjected to her small, oppressive bedsit at the Langham, no, Sara will voyage to America. She will voyage to a better life on the other side of the pond. And she *will* be happy.

Or will she be?

After informing both her unsupportive mother and her imperialistic boss at the Langham of her new job offer in the developing U.S., Sara sets sail on her voyage to the good old land of opportunity.

Oh, if things were only so simple and easy.

NEW YORK CITY, 1985.

Fresh out of a fancy rehabilitation clinic (a stay that was funded by her employer), Bailey Camden, possibly a fourth-generation descendant of the renowned Theo Camden via Sara Smythe's womb, is a gifted interior designer who battles with her own personal demons of alcoholism and drug addiction. After humiliating not only herself but also an honored client of the design firm for which she works, Bailey is fired by her distinguished boss and left out on the street with nothing of value to cushion her unexpected downfall. Enter Melinda Camden, Bailey's so-called cousin, and a young woman who is as ignorant as she is arrogant. Melinda, having knowledge of Bailey's dire plight, offers her "lessor" relative a job—in addition to free room and board—at the *Dakota*, which, by the way, is now under the authority of the greedy, spoiled, hateful, spiteful, and materialistic Melinda. Bailey's job duties would include updating the famed property from its classic Gilded Age decor to tacky and unsophisticated ornamentation, much to the disdain of the building's current residents. Incidentally, *Dakota* has become a co-op. And not all are pleased with it in its current state.

In only a matter of days—when they turn 30 years of age—both the covetous Melinda and her twin brother, Manvil, stand to inherit millions from the Camden family trust. But what about the cash-poor and down-on-her-luck

Bailey? She's a Camden too, right? Her great-grandfather Christopher, who was the lovechild of Theo Camden and Sara Smythe, and the father of Bailey's father, Jack, had a right to the legacy—which was to be divided among all the heirs of Theo Camden—too, right? Yes, that's right. But who is entitled and who is not entitled to the fortune will all boil down to the male bloodline.

Who is the real Camden? Melinda or Bailey? Who truly has a right to the multi-million dollar estate?

Who really murdered Theo Camden?

While searching through all of the old trunks hidden away and forgotten in the basement storage container at the *Dakota*, Bailey finds treasures in the vintage personal effects of not only Theo Camden but also his widow, Minnie, and Sara Smythe. And these hidden treasures can prove, beyond the shadow of a doubt, that Bailey is indeed a Camden by blood, and not just symbolically.

With the help of Renzo, who just so happens to be the building's superintendent and Melinda's archenemy, Bailey sets out to determine her findings by law, through DNA, much to the disdain of her so-called cousin, Melinda. And the revelation will shock them all.

OVER A CENTURY OF ELEGANCE.

Graced with an elegant storyline full of twists and turns, not to mention a splendid cast of unforgettable characters, *The Address* is fast-paced and engrossing from start to finish. It is one of those rare reads that you'll hate to put down or be away from too long. And no lover of historical fiction should have his or her bookshelf void of it.

On the pages of *The Address*, the talented Fiona Davis transports her readers from the nineteenth century to the twentieth-century in a mind-blowing tale brimming with love, lust, hatred, deceit, ravenous cunning, bitter jealousy, and heartbreaking brutality. Especially challenging to read were the stories about the inhumane treatments suffered by the inmates at Blackwell's Island Asylum.

A gorgeous work of literary art, *The Address* is destined for legendary status. And just as I regretted concluding it, I'm nearly certain that many other readers will as well; therefore, I highly recommend *The Address* as it is a novel very commendable.

Five gilded stars.

Cat Ellington's Review of Size Zero by A.C. Moyer

My rating: 5 out of 5 stars

Date read: May 2017

IS BEAUTY ONLY SKIN DEEP?

The concept of that adage may ring true for some, but in many cases, when the subject factors around the innermost soul of man, it can be downright ugly . . . and evil.

Trust that the reader, after viewing A.C. Moyer's somewhat eerie *Size Zero*, will never again look at the high-fashion industry in quite the same way. Trust that the reader, in the wake of concluding this tale, will never again look at the glamorous models who strut the runways of Milan, Paris, and New York Fashion Week, in quite the same way. Trust that the reader, after completing this ferocious anecdote, will never again look at the coveted models whose beautiful faces grace the glossy covers of high-fashion magazines in quite the same way.

BEARING THE TRUTH.

Masterfully-written by the smart-as-a-whip Moyer, *Size Zero* is a brutal, bile-in-the-throat tale that overflows with self-loathing, perversity, and depravity, and snatches the rug back to expose the spirit of immorality that dwells in those so-called gatekeepers of the high-fashion industry.

Walking the tightrope of truth over a canyon of scorching lava—like a natural-born Wallenda—Moyer presents a scandalous script that puts the degeneracy of the fashion industry, including its high-end luxuries, under an unflinching microscope while paying a great deal of attention to a perfectly-hemmed dialogue and expertly-stitched character development.

APPLAUDING A GREAT VISION.

With *Size Zero*, A.C. Moyer morphs nonfiction with fiction in such a remarkable way, that its content will leave you in absolute awe. The effort was created as the result of tremendous fieldwork done on the part of its author; and because of this, she is wholly deserving of my commendation.

Starring Cecil LeClaire and Ava Germaine—who both render outstanding performances—the narrative is ingenuine in delivery and rapid in pace. And with an ending that will leave your psyche drenched in a dark, semi-sweet scent reminiscent of Bvlgari's Jasmin Noir, *Size Zero*—five-star fabulous, to say the least—is a must-read if you just so happen to be a fashion industry enthusiast.

Five fashion-conscious stars.

Cat Ellington's Review of Dark Harvest (A Holt Foundation Story Book 2) by Chris Patchell

My rating: 5 out of 5 stars

Date read: May 2017

SEATTLE'S BEST ... AND WORST.

Teen pregnancies, kidnappings, unborn fetus harvesting, illegal adoptions, emotional hardships, cold and dreary days soaked in rain, human trafficking, sex trafficking, love lost, love won, cold-blooded murders, fiery explosions, scars—of both the mental and physical type—illogical medical madness, and the forcible will to live all contribute to the gripping suspense on the pages of this enthralling mystery thriller.

Author Chris Patchell does a sublime job with *Dark Harvest*!

Loaded with tons of twists and turns, the poignant narrative—set in beautiful Seattle—features an intriguing, however problematic, cast of characters that are each deeply unsettled in their individual lives. The troupe about whom I speak are as follows:

• Marissa Rooney, former teen mother and our leading lady. Marissa's life is a barrel of self-doubt and conflict that stems from her youth.

• Seth Crawford, a troubled former cop and Marissa's boyfriend. While he loves and protects Marissa, Seth still battles with many demons from his past.

• Brooke, Marissa's youngest daughter. The teenaged Brooke survived a horrible ordeal at the hands of a deranged psychopath—the same psychopath who murdered her best friend—and is struggling to return to a place of normalcy in her young life.

• Kelly, Marissa's eldest daughter. The teenaged Kelly wasn't given a broad role in this great, cinematic novel, but her contribution is still valuable, nevertheless.

• Henry, a brilliant computer hacker at the Holt Foundation. Henry is not only a genius coder but also an annoying thorn in Seth Crawford's side.

• Evan Holt, Holt Foundation heir, and boss to Marissa, Seth, and Henry. Evan Holt has summoned his best team to work together—though they do so on haphazard terms with the Seattle P.D.—to find two missing pregnant women who have been identified as Becky Kincaid and Suzie Norwood.

• Dr. Xander Wilcox, an esteemed mastermind of a surgeon. Dr. Xander Wilcox is also a cancerous tumor on the integrity of the medical profession.

- Victoria "Tory" Kaplan, Dr. Xander Wilcox's pretty, young nurse. Deserving of both pity and contempt, Victoria Kaplan is a stunning redhead who plays her part well as a hapless man-pleaser and a dastardly partner to Dr. Xander Wilcox.

IN ACCLAMATION.

Chris Patchell wraps this compelling ensemble around a plot so thrilling, unnerving, and mystifying, that it will keep the reader engrossed from beginning to end. *Dark Harvest* is blessed with an ending so well-written and enrapturing, that the reader won't even realize they've concluded it until they turn the final page and see the *Author's Notes*. That's just how entertaining *Dark Harvest* is. It will leave you wanting more. I was loath to complete this dialogue but I had to, unfortunately, although not without shedding a few tears.

Greatly recommended, *Dark Harvest* is a wonderful effort to enjoy over a quiet weekend. And of it, Chris Pratchell—its creative mother—should be extremely proud.

Five troubled stars.

Cat Ellington's Review of The Switch by Joseph Finder

My rating: 4 out of 5 stars

Date read: May 2017

MEET JOSEPH FINDER.

Immediately after signing up to become a new member of the Penguin Random House First to Read program, I was provided with an intriguing bundle of upcoming titles that were being offered as Advanced Review Copies (ARCs) with the request option to view. And this intriguing bundle of imminent titles included *The Switch*, the latest thriller from author Joseph Finder.

Taken not only by the book's cover art but also its fascinating description, I requested a galley proof of *The Switch* and received an approval notification less than 72 hours later. And boy, am I glad I did. Because no sooner had I started reading this title than I became completely submerged in its conspiratorial plot.

It certainly lives up to its description.

WICKED INTENTIONS.

Set in Boston, Massachusetts, and Washington D.C., *The Switch* is a twisted political thriller packed with fear, paranoia, anxiety, and frustration. Indeed, this latest effort from Joseph Finder gives a whole new meaning to the old phrase, 'Big Brother Is Watching You.'

The madness begins to unfold when, while going through the checkpoint at LAX, a coffee executive named Michael Tanner—who just so happens to be our leading man—collects and repacks his effects, including an exorbitant MacBook Air, right before he boards his flight home to Boston. However, there is one problem: Michael Tanner – "Tanner" to his loved ones, including his estranged wife, Sarah – in his haste to get home, has picked up the wrong MacBook Air with his personal belongings. Unbeknownst to the beloved Michael Tanner, The MacBook Air in his possession belongs to a very important—*and very powerful*—woman named Susan Robbins. An enthusiast of Nina Ricci's *L'Air du Temps*, the pleasantly-scented Susan Robbins is a United States Senator with a great deal of political influence. And her laptop, the same laptop that is now in Michael Tanner's possession, contains top-secret government documents not intended for public knowledge. Tanner doesn't know it yet, but should he open the ill-fated MacBook Air and acquire knowledge of its confidential data, not only will his life be in grave danger but also the lives of tens of millions of other Americans.

It isn't until Michael Tanner returns home, that he realizes his error of grabbing the wrong laptop at LAX. When he powers on the computer and sees the pink post-it icon indicating the name of the laptop's owner to be one S. Robbins, Tanner knows he goofed up. But when he notices

S. Robbins' government-issued password right there on the home screen, of course, our leading man can't help but be curious.

Probing further, Tanner signs in to the owner's account and discovers that S. Robbins is none other than Senator Susan Robbins. Because his curiosity won't leave him be, Michael Tanner goes on to read the horrifying documents on the laptop in detail. And upon completion, his expected reaction is sheer fear. Straight away, Tanner calls his close friend, Lanny, who is not only a conspiracy theorist but also a well-respected journalist for *The Boston Globe*. And after Tanner shares every detail of the documents, not to mention copies of the hard drive, with Lanny, the plot of this tale, as if being infused with cornstarch, begins to thicken.

GIVE IT BACK!

Everyone—from the self-loathing Will Abbott to Senator Susan Robbins to the National Security Agency to a former Marine naval infantryman—is now on the hunt for Michael Tanner. They all want that loaded laptop back. And they *will* get it back from Michael Tanner, even if they have to kill him, or his loved ones, to do so.

Michael Tanner's once peaceful, comfortable, and lovable life has been turned upside down and inside out. And he's now on the run for his life. But just how far will he get? In Michael Tanner's new reality of conspiracy, espionage, contract murders, double-dealing, and invasive technology, the question is, Who will outwit who?

THE COMPARISON.

Michael Tanner is to *The Switch* what "Mitch McDeere" is to Grisham's legendary legal thriller, *The Firm*, except that Michael Tanner may very well be a fictional stand-in for the scandalous Edward Snowden. It's easy to assume, considering that more than a few sections in this tale reference both WikiLeaks and the now famous—or infamous, depending on whom you ask—whistleblower.

Although not as intense as Grisham's *The Firm*—due to some much slower parts here and there—*The Switch* still does its job of keeping the reader engrossed, even up to its cliffhanger ending.

RESPECTFULLY RECOMMENDED.

What could have easily been a five-star rating is foiled - only because I felt that the narrative was sputtering a bit along the way. Overall, *The Switch* is well-written and entertaining in its own right. And I would highly recommend it to those readers who can appreciate a good political thriller.

LASTLY.

Is Joseph Finder's *The Switch* keen on detail, research, and character evolution? Undeniably.

Is *The Switch* an enjoyable roman à clef that I would be happy to add to my vast collection of thrillers in every subgenre? Most definitely.

Happy reading, all.

Bonus Material by Naras Kimono

Naras Kimono's Review of Dog Facts by Joan Palmer

Rating: 5 out of 5 stars

Date read: September 2015

Because I'm such a dog lover, my daddy gave me *Dog Facts* as a gift on Election Day last year. Excited, I went into my bedroom, climbed into my bed, and started reading. And I loved the book right away. As I turned the pages, I started to see many different kinds of dog breeds that I've never seen before or even knew existed. But the breed I loved the most was the German Shepherd. The German Shepherd is my favorite dog breed of them all. And I read all of the details about it over and over and over again. My mother doesn't like German Shepherds, but I do. I think they're tough, and they're very protective of their families. And if there is anyone like me who loves this breed, they will love all of the information about it in Ms. Palmer's *Dog Facts*.

I'm working on my own book about dogs, and *Dog Facts* gave me some great ideas for my research – like the Hound group page for example, particularly the Dachshund. If you're a Dachshund lover, *Dog Facts* features three types of Dachshunds: the wire-haired, the long-haired, and the smooth-haired. There are also many other breeds that dog lovers like myself are sure to love, including the Chinese Crested, the Cocker Spaniel, the Shar-Pei, the Yorkshire Terrier, the Dalmatian, the Doberman, the Rottweiler, etc.

The book also includes sections dedicated to the nature of the canine in general, including Inoculation and Health Care, Neuterings and Spayings, Canine Disorders, Caring for Elderly Canines, and more. There is even a Breeds of the World Introduction that I found very fascinating as it lists every dog breed from around the globe.

An overall encyclopedia, Joan Palmer's *Dog Facts* is a must-have and a must-read. And every dog lover in the world should own a copy of it.
That's my review. I love *Dog Facts* by Joan Palmer. And I give it five stars.

Now on to "Dog Tales."

Publisher's Note:

This review of *Dog Facts* by Joan Palmer was written by Naras Kimono at age 11. It has been edited for clarity.

Naras Kimono's Review of Pinkalicious: Tickled Pink by Victoria Kann

Rating: 5 out of 5 stars

Date read: October 2014

Today, I read *Pinkalicious: Tickled Pink* by Victoria Kann. In this story, our lead character, Pinkalicious, goes to her local library in search of a good book to read. She soon finds a book with a bright pink cover and shiny gold letters titled, *The Goofy Book of Gags and Giggles.* And when she opens the book, she sees that it is full of hilarious jokes. Pinkalicious then shares the jokes in the library book with her readers. And I couldn't stop laughing at all the funny punchlines as I read along with them. Molly, Pinkalicious's best friend, couldn't stop laughing either as Pinkalicious read the jokes in *The Goofy Book of Gags and Giggles* to her.

Tiffany, a foe of Pinkalicious and Molly, is standing around listening in, getting angrier at the two best friends with every good moment they share, just laughing together. Tiffany then imposes herself on them and challenges Pinkalicious to a laugh-off. After she accuses Pinkalicious of not having 'a real funny bone in her body,' Tiffany then dares the popular Pinkalicious to come up with some of her *own* jokes. And with all of the other kids watching on and listening, Pinkalicious, now put on the spot, has no other choice but to accept Tiffany's challenge. And with that, the pressure is on to create the most pinkerrifically funny joke of all time.

But can she do it? Can Pinkalicious beat that mean girl Tiffany at her own game? Will she be able to bowl all of her friends (and foes) over with the funniest joke any of them have ever heard?

All of the Pinkalicious fans are sure to find out on these crazy pages of pinkerrific fun!

Pinkalicious: Tickled Pink is a great book centered around bullying, peer pressure, self-esteem, self-doubt, courage, and confidence. And it is a book that I would recommend to kids – like myself – who take pleasure in seeing the good guys win.

I had fun reading *Pinkalicious: Tickled Pink,* and I'm so glad that I own a copy of it.

I give it five stars.

Publisher's Note:

This review of *Pinkalicious: Tickled Pink* by Victoria Kann was written by Naras Kimono at age 10. It has been edited for clarity.

Naras Kimono's Review of Eye to Eye with Dogs: Dachshunds by Lynn M. Stone

Rating: 5 out of 5 stars

Date read: September 2015

I just finished reading Lynn M. Stone's *Eye to Eye with Dogs: Dachshunds,* and I loved it! Packed with a ton of information about the three varieties of Dachshund, including the longhaired, the wirehaired, and the shorthaired, the book taught me even more than I already know about this breed that I'm so crazy about. For education purposes, the reference provides the reader with a detailed biography of the Dachshund breed, and I couldn't take notes fast enough.

I learned that the name Dachshund, translated in German, means "Badger Dog." And I also learned why. For many years, these cute little members of the hound group were used by their breeders to hunt badgers. And in time, the Dachshund became one of the most popular purebred dog breeds in North America.

Because of their frankfurter-like bodies – with their deep chest and short legs – Dachshunds are commonly referred to as 'Wieners' or 'Hot Dogs.' And because they tend to be "yippy," Dachshunds make excellent watchdogs—though their excessive barking may not always go over well with their humans.

In addition to the treasure trove of information about their heritage and personalities, Lynn M. Stone also educates his Dachshund-loving readers with details about kennel club registrations and rankings, standard facts about weight and height, life expectancy rates, a glossary of word pronunciations, etc.

I loved *Eye to Eye with Dogs: Dachshunds*. And I would recommend reading it to anyone who has an interest in learning more about this breed. Thank you, Mr. Stone! This reference book helped to expand my knowledge about the Dachshund, and I will keep it forever.

I give *Eye to Eye with Dogs: Dachshunds* five stars.

Publisher's Note:

This review of *Eye to Eye with Dogs: Dachshunds* by Lynn M. Stone was written by Naras Kimono at age 11. It has been edited for clarity.

Coming Soon

Reviews by Cat Ellington: The Complete Anthology, Vol. 5
Imprint: Quill Pen Ink Publishing
Cover Hue: Ultraviolet

About the Authors

Cat Ellington is an American songwriter, casting director, poet, and author from Chicago, IL. She is best known for her creative contributions to the diverse industries and fields of music, movies, art, and literature.

Outside of her professional element, the award-winning lyricist enjoys reading, listening to music, cooking, collecting vintage and modern charm bracelets, watching LMN, film noir movies, and classic TV shows, sailing, jet skiing, playing tennis, and eating lots of frozen yogurt.

Cat Ellington lives in Chicago with her husband Joseph Strickland, their three children Nathaniel, Nairobi, and Naras, and the family's pet Pomeranian, Aspen.

<u>Cat Ellington on Amazon: Books, Biography, Blog, Audiobooks, Kindle</u>

<u>Cat Ellington at the Award-Winning Boutique Domain</u>

<u>Cat Ellington at the Review Period with Cat Ellington</u>

<u>Cat Ellington at IMDb</u>

Naras Kimono (born Naras Kimono Strickland on August 23, 2004) is an American author and artist from Chicago, IL. She has been writing short stories and illustrating graphics since she was very young, and made her professional writing debut as a contributing author on the fourth installment of the Reviews by Cat Ellington book series.

When she's not writing, creating characters, or drawing, Naras enjoys reading, watching Nickelodeon, studying dog breeds, cooking, listening to music, drinking chai tea, and engaging in various outdoor activities.

Naras Kimono lives in Chicago with her parents Joseph Strickland and Cat Ellington, her two brothers Nathaniel Joseph and Nairobi Kenya, and the family's pet Pomeranian, Aspen.

Naras Kimono on Amazon: Books, Biography, Blog, Audiobooks, Kindle

Naras Kimono at the Award-Winning Boutique Domain

Naras Kimono at Goodreads

Naras Kimono at BookBub

Naras Kimono at AUTHORSdb

Naras Kimono at LibraryThing

Naras Kimono at Open Library

Naras Kimono at IMDb

www.ingramcontent.com/pod-product-compliance
Lightning Source LLC
Chambersburg PA
CBHW031357040426
42444CB00005B/323